THE
HUMAN SPIRIT

BY

ANN REE COLTON

ARC PUBLISHING COMPANY
POST OFFICE BOX 1138
GLENDALE, CALIFORNIA 91209

Second Printing, 1977

Printed in the United States of America
BOOK GRAPHICS, INC.
Marina del Rey, CA 90291

This book
is
dedicated
To those who serve
The need of the world,
To those who heal the sick,
Who give peace to the confused,
Who instruct the spiritually impoverished,
And to those who pray to become
Mediative Healers.

ACKNOWLEDGMENTS

I wish to express my gratitude to my devoted associate, Jonathan Murro, for his untiring guidance and assistance. His inspired editing has been a necessary strength supplementing my efforts throughout the years.

I also wish to give thanks for additional editing helps received from my beloved friends, Anastasia Wilson, Alban McRoberts, Serena Burris, and Tobias DeMarchi.

CONTENTS

1　Prelude　.　.　.　.　.　.　.　.　.　1

2　Cosmic Birth　.　.　.　.　.　.　.　17

3　Birth of the Earth　.　.　.　.　.　.　.　31

4　The Bodies of Man　.　.　.　.　.　.　.　43

5　Tribes and Races　.　.　.　.　.　.　.　62

6　Prototypes　.　.　.　.　.　.　.　.　94

7　Family-Atom　.　.　.　.　.　.　.　.　113

8　Marriage and the Family　.　.　.　.　.　136

9　Self-Genesis　.　.　.　.　.　.　.　.　157

10　Initiation　.　.　.　.　.　.　.　.　.　177

11　Ethic and Healing　.　.　.　.　.　.　.　200

12　Mediative Healing　.　.　.　.　.　.　.　213

13　Healing Technique and Mantrams　.　.　.　234

　　Index　.　.　.　.　.　.　.　.　.　.　278

　　List of Other Books　.　.　.　.　.　.　290

1

PRELUDE

*He who speaketh the word "brother,"
and doeth unto his brother as he would not
have his brother do unto him, knoweth not
the human spirit. He who would abuse his
fellow man, that he might profit from
his fellow man, knoweth not the human
spirit. He who is filled with the higher
ideals of the human spirit seeth eye to
eye with his brother, and looketh to the
common gain or goal through righteousness. There shall come the day in which the
human spirit shall enter into the hearts and
minds of men. This is God's ideation for
man. This is God's manifestation for man.*

The human spirit presses to be born in all
men. In the birth of the human spirit, the heart
of each man is searched. The Light of the Christ
searches the minds of men; and the Love of
God prepares to reign in the lives of men.

The Will of God is compelling man to incorporate into his soul the soul-uniqueness of
other men. Man is being forced to relinquish
his mortal aloneness, that he may discover and
live close to the illimitable powers of his soul.

The Love of God in all men waits to be

manifested. Man, in spiritual dryness, is as timber which awaits the flame and fire of God. The fire of God will warm him, purify him, cleanse him, and bring him to a day of worthiness.

There is a spiritual solution to each problem for the individual; there is also a spiritual solution for mass upheavals. The solution for mass upheavals takes generations of time, while individual problems relate to day by day. Enlightened souls have attained a widened perspective of the human spirit. One who has sacrificed unites his individual aim with the composite spiritual destiny for all men.

Long has been the pilgrimage of man. Ages upon ages men have struggled to rise in the world. Until the struggle becomes joy, and the desire for enlightenment wholly consumes the mind, men will suffer. Some in the world know not the difference between the twilight action of mediocrity and a glorious mind illumined of God. They have yet to learn that inspiration and the power of spiritual imaging may be attained only through the love of God, the love of life, the love of one's fellow man.

Every human soul is responsible to his fellow soul or brother. His fears and hates afflict those who breathe with him in the world. His love and trust unite him with those who love as he loves.

Men who foresee and anticipate the birth of the human spirit work with love continually. They give birth in their hearts to the vision of an immortal man-to-be—a man who will stand with the Christ and make the earth into a holy crucible. They will bring to starry birth the earth's continents. When the starry birth has come to the continents, it will touch the world and the planets. The earth will become a sea of light from which a mighty star will be born; and there will be a song in galaxy—for a cosmic earth will have become a spiritual sun.

The divisions, tumults, and unrest in the world today are due to the birth of the human spirit. Forceful, agnostic, and unknowing men—failing to respond to the greater spiritual impulses—are resisting the upsurge of refinement and evolvement for man. Unknowing men dream their days away during great spiritual impulses. Agnostic men respond to the greater spiritual impulses by caustically and cynically withdrawing their hearts from their fellow men. Forceful men incite men to wars, and thus unwittingly act as negative catalysts to move and change the decadent separative patterns of mankind.

Men are pressured, that their vision may extend into new horizons. They are offended, that they may better hear what God is saying to them inwardly. They are cast upon new shores, that they may merge with the soul nuances of other men. They are placed into positions of labors and crafts which will widen their views and concepts of the universe.

Science, with its space discoveries, will prove the Eternal Spirit. Science will also confirm man's immortal soul. However, man will be the true discovery, for the human-spirit man will be placed under a new microscope. He will know not only himself, but he will also know his fellow man—and in his knowing, he will revere him, and he will devote his efforts to lifting his fellow man as well as himself.

God, the Eternal One, saith unto man: "Arise, and enter thou into the finer substances of love and peace." The Spirit of God is ensouled in the human spirit. The human spirit saith unto man: "Arise, and look unto thy brother with love."

Since the coming of the Lord Jesus, the human spirit has increased its quickening, moving, rising. When man has attained the noble aspects of the human spirit, the Spirit of God shall glorify him. The human spirit shall produce the creative man. Man will recognize the right of his fellow man to experience, to love, to act; and more—to seek God. When the human spirit has attained its crown, men will receive the Divine Spirit—the Christ.

Until the coming of Jesus, the human spirit

was in its fetal state. The human spirit, overdirected by the Race Lord Jehovah, was expressed through tribes, races, and families. The human spirit now seeks to blend nations and continents, placing emphasis upon a *world conscience* supporting the rights of the individual soul of man.

God's perfect timing produced Jesus, the perfect catalyst to free men into their true heritage, that their souls might unite with the souls of other men. When the human spirit is fulfilled, the soul of each man will speak to the soul of his fellow man.

The earth is moving toward the time in which man will think of his fellow man as he formerly thought of persons in his family or home.

The velocity and quickening of this accelerated age have produced negative, destroyer-titan persons to disassemble old communities, habits, standards, and ideas. Men may now look to ethical and prescient souls sent of God to the earth. These noble and pure souls will give insight into greater goals, that the Father's Plan may be established in the world. Such persons will make men aware of the power of Divine Mediation, and teach them certain rules by which the doors of Heaven are kept open.

Men who offend the human spirit reap the tares of ignorance, doubt, and separateness. When the human spirit is offended, wars come unto men. When the human spirit is defiled, calamities come unto men. When the human spirit is yet unseen and unknown by men, hates are nourished, and prejudices are manifold. The human spirit, in this day, works that man may build a nobler body, a nobler mind, and an ethic through which his emotions shall no longer bruise him or offend his brother.

If a cell be sick in the body, an organ becomes faulty; if an organ becomes faulty, the body becomes impaired and sick. In human society, when one person stands selfishly alone, he is a sickness unto himself and to society. When men no longer believe themselves to be sufficient unto themselves, the Spirit of God will enter their thoughts and teach them.

God gave to all creatures the power of love. Only in man is found the abuse of love. To distort love or to make terms with love violates the soul's most sacred attribute—love. Materialistic men express self-love and self-preservation. Advanced egos, or the Elect of the earth, express the godly aspect of love.

Man's survival in the earth, and in all earths-to-be, depends solely on his capacity to love. He who loves life cherishes all things in the light of love.

The human spirit and the Eternal One would make each man responsible. When thou teachest the weak to lift themselves, thou becomest stronger, and thou makest them stronger—and thou risest with the momentum of thy strength. Thou livest not for that one who is weak, but thou teachest him to set up the momentum of life within. He who giveth hope to the weak giveth the way on which the restoring life cometh forth. Through this, the burdens of the world are lifted, and the human spirit may begin to speak unto man. Teach each man to aid himself, and teach each man to aid his brother. Teach him to turn not away from that which is needed in the aid of his brother.

In the beginning of this earth, man was given a conscience through which God and His angels could speak. Conscience made him a perceiver of the two alternatives: good and evil. Through choice, man could choose whether he responded to the voice of God speaking through his conscience or to the voice of his cowardice, doubts, and fears. Regardless of his liberty to choose, his conscience walked with him as a troublesome mentor and reminder.

When man chose to respond to the voice of his angels, his conscience, over the aeons, gradually became a reliable and trustworthy aspect of his soul—protecting and supporting his works of good. Those who did not choose to respond to the voice of their consciences were the Cains of the world who preferred to experiment through the sense-action level of their physical natures. While prospering at the ex-

pense of the naive in the world, their wills
became hardened against the Will of God—and
they became stiffnecked or agnostic. The sensual
side of their natures became their God. They
extended their lust from generation to generation, and they crowded the earth with the
progeny of their pollutions.

The Will of God is immutable. His law has
been set in the earth. The greater Recording
Angels and mighty Judgment Angels record
the good and the evil existing in the earth.
When the axis pole of the earth becomes over-
burdened with the soil of man's selfishness, great
cataclysms come to the earth; wars are insti-
gated; famines and plagues afflict men. These
devastating negativities purge the earth, modu-
lating and tempering the stubborn wills of men.

*In the birth of the human spirit, inertia and
indifference are as small stones sleeping beneath
an avalanche. Inertia is being energized into
new vitalities. Indifference is to be stripped of
its cynicism and self-sufficiency. Those who
resist the birth of the human spirit will be
sculptured by the Hand of God, as the tidal
wave of new birth now sweeps men upward
into greater skills and greater crafts.*

All pain and sorrow of the mind are caused
by a feeling of detachment from the love of
God. The weighty burdens of racial, family, and
personal conscience, placed upon the shoulders

of man, produce a carnal heaviness in some, a
rugged virtue in others, and a noble dignity in
those who have insight into spiritual law and
its resultant good.

In man's most primitive or tribal states, he
is protected by the blessing of being endowed
with a conscience overdirected by the Guardian
Angel of his tribe. In the life of a family, the
conscience is overdirected by the Guardian
Angel of the family. In the life of the highly
evolved individual, his personal Guardian
Angel directs and supervises his conscience, that
he may unite his conscience with the world
conscience. Heretofore, men have intuited that
God is ensouled in all things. When individual
conscience has united with world conscience,
man will *know* that God is in him, in his
brother—and that all things of the world are
truly of God.

To see eye to eye and soul to soul with one's
fellow man is to be generous with him; to teach
him, if he be awkward; to lift him, if he be
weak; to be patient with him, if he be dull or
laggard. How may the Risen Christ lift men,
when men agree with their oppressors, and
when men agree to oppress other men? How
may the human spirit overflow into men, save
each man free other men in the world? How
may the world express creation with ethic, save
men learn to understand the meaning of crafts-

manship? How may men become pure and live within the whole in God, save they first make pure their hearts, their minds, their bodies, their works? One should learn of these things, and remember that men grow in stature when they overcome pain and oppression; he should also know that men transcend these things through Christ.

The happiest state of existence man may know is to see God's creation in the hearts, skills, and labors of his fellow craftsman and fellow man.

The very special uniqueness or signature of the master craftsman is supported by an invisible asset inherited from all craftsmen who have gone before him. The motives of a true craftsman are energized by a godly vitality.

The crafts of men are rooted in three basic expressions: builders, shepherds, and scientists. From these crafts stem many tributary outlets or impulses. If man is a builder, his spiritual nature inspires him to erect better and better structures, esthetically appealing to the eye; dramatically testifying to God, the Builder. The ethical builder for men is aware that he is a mediative channel for creation. He is stimulated by the miraculous ways in which the unexpected soul-versatilities of other men assist him and strengthen him.

A spiritual builder unites himself with many resources invisible to other men; the true builder draws upon the powerful creative fiats of God. To plant the seed of inspiration in another is to receive a reward of grace, providing soul skills and techniques which give voice to the handiwork of God.

A shepherd of men is a healer, a teacher, a philosopher, a leader. He works with the mercy aspect in creation. He knows the right time to lead the weak into more verdant pastures. He is a revivifier of the physical, moral, and spiritual health of men. He uses the potencies of his wisdom and the flexibilities of his intuition to lift and to heal men. His wisdom soothes away their phantasies. He teaches them to look with honest insight into their own natures, and thus reap the rewards of a mercy grace or charitableness from other men.

The shepherd-creator stands in grace. His burden is lifted and lightened through grace. He leads through example, tenderness, cheer, truth, justice. The true shepherd observes without judgment. He knows that each person must be willing to accept the changes and transitions within his soul nature and human nature. The shepherd must ever be ready to assist one with the load when it is heavy, and to relinquish the yoke when the one who follows him is born to his own creation and strength.

The scientist dares to probe the unknown. He explores the little-known facets of man's routine and regulated world. He upsets and agitates complacency. His ideas are resented and mis-understood, for he dares to bring new truths, new concepts, new conclusions. The scientist is a creative prover for God. The true scientist is impartial in his research and conclusions. He has a patience equal to his thirst for knowledge. He protects the non-receptive minds of men, even while he frees them from the shackles of their crystallized neglects.

The builder, the shepherd, and the scientist, when supreme creators for God, gather knowl-edge and wisdom from the generations of the past, and give vision and hope to generations to come.

This is an age daring men to excel. Creative exuberances challenge men to share their ex-cellence, to give the uttermost rather than the least.

The human spirit seeks to be embodied with-in the body of man. The human spirit works that it may regenerate the creative souls of the many. The Eternal One dwells within each loving heart. He looks to the time in which the human spirit shall mature, and give stature, nobility, and dignity to man. The love of spir-itually enlightened men supports the soul needs of humankind. Loving, illumined men work with the generation-grace of the ages.

When the human spirit has established the

world conscience, a fourth-dimensional craftsman will come to the world—a craftsman who
will be engrossed in the study of the soul-origin
and soul-potential of man. Men have used the
word "soul" loosely, not knowing its complete
function. The perfected craftsman of the
human spirit will be a combination of builder,
shepherd, and scientist. He shall be so rooted
within the vine of the Son of Man, or Jesus,
that he will incite a cosmos metamorphosis in
the souls of others; he will be an eternal man
inhabiting an eternity. Having ripened and
matured through the ages, he will express the
immortal tone of love. He will embody a versatile composite of ethics on all levels of human
association. His mentality will draw upon the
higher ethos of humanity, and he will give
formulas to soften the harsher aspects in human
nature. He will have unobstructed access to
the compendium of the spiritual archetypes or
greater ideas stemming from God. His religious
impulses will be stimulated by the sacraments
and sanctuaries of Heaven. He will unceasingly
worship God. The power of imaging within his
mental logos will unite him with the mighty
builders—the hosts or Hierarchs of the universe. He will partake of the Father's table, and
sit as a son at the feast or agape of God. He will
walk with the Lord Jesus—touching the polarities, continents, nations. As a spiritual healer, he

will divine with a holy intuition the needs of struggling men. He will see that man's unknowing keeps alive the sins of the world. He will be a knower-craftsman, a creative craftsman. He will hear God, and instantaneously respond to His Word.

The fourth-dimensional craftsman of the human spirit will be like the Jesus One. Aeons will pass before this ideal man will be the common denominator among men. At rare intervals, great men will come who aspire to be like Jesus. God sends such souls to the world as holy seeds to implant in man new hope, new vision.

Until the human spirit has reached its ultimate, men will make mistakes, and learn. They will err, and suffer. They will try, and fail. However, through the eternal timing as given of God, they will inevitably bring to birth a man of worth under God.

The Eternal One and the human spirit work to produce new heart-themes in men, and new creative impulses in the soul of humanity. The human spirit uses for its body the continents of the earth. That which man calls "the self" uses the human body; the human spirit uses the earth as a body. Let all mankind come forth within their continents, and be crowned by the Sovereign of the human spirit—the Lord Jesus. Let the human spirit come to birth. And let it increase above the pain and pangs of birth. Let

the human spirit be united with the Light of
the Christ. If men will turn to the Christ, they
will enter into a painless birth of the human
spirit. When men turn their faces from the
Christ, their pain, labor and travail are long.
Let men see the Christ as the Son of God, as
the only begotten Son of God—and let them
know Him in the Light.

There are no superior or inferior persons,
races, or nations. To think of a fellow man as
inferior is to demean humanity. Men, who refuse to know, choose the way of unknowing
because they grow and evolve more slowly in
the tempo of their souls. Such men remain
rooted to the primitive side of their wills. Those
who have accelerated response to the inner wisdom of the eternals move in quickened tempo
to their souls' direction.

God gives to man the freedom of will to set
his own pace, his own timing. The soul of a race
decides its pace in development. The soul of a
nation determines its pace and placement among
nations.

The original soul theme of each person in the
world is sacredly different. Each person responds to God as he feels and knows God to be.

In the beginning of the great aeons, God established for man a number of supra-assistances
to support his life on earth. God gave the chemicals within the earth to provide for man his

energies, his medicines, his nourishments. He gave to man the minerals through mountains, soils, and ores. He gave to man the seas, the creatures and plants within the seas. He gave him the springs, the lakes, the rivers. He gave him the plants with their verdant fertility. He gave man the animals for companions to serve him, and to make more tender his compassion. He gave him the angels and the holy presences to comfort, strengthen, and guide him. And lastly, He gave to man His Son to be the Mediator between man and the Kingdom of Heaven.

Charitable thoughts toward one's fellow man are increased and vitalized when one praises God and sees His Eternal Spirit ensouled in the chemical, in the mountain, in the ocean, in the plant, in the animal, in his fellow man. When one has the grace to behold the angels in their celestial forms, and is aware of heavenly Mediation, there can be no separateness between him and any form of life. He feels and knows an awesome reverence for all persons, beings, things. He is thrice blessed—and he walks with God.

2

COSMIC BIRTH

The Spirit of God giveth life; the Spirit of God moveth upon the hidden deep.

The Word of God soundeth, and life cometh forth.

The Might of God is witnessed in His beginnings, His endings.

The Presence of God is manifested through His universes, His eternities, His angels, His mediators.

The Will of God is spiritual, celestial, terrestrial.

The Love of God is eternal tenderness.

The Life of God is ceaseless germination, unending creation.

The Law of God is concealed in miracles, wisdoms, and mysteries.

The Equation of God defines and decides.

The Works of God are disclosed through His Elect, His craftsmen.

The Light of God is the animating consciousness centered within all mentalities, sentient and omniscient.

The Power of God transcends all evil.

The Judgment of God replenishes and retrieves the soul.

The universe is filled with stars, galaxies, and eternity systems—all moving to the pace of God's Equation. Their beginnings and their endings are determined and timed by the Will of God.

To understand birth, one must turn not to the woman who held him in the cradle of her womb, but he must turn to the womb of the eternal cosmos where eternities are born.

The starry atmosphere is the bosom of God. The Spirit of God moves and creates. God is Light. His Spirit generates the highest degree of light when eternity systems undergo death and rebirth. As infants are being born every second in the earth, eternity systems in starry cosmos are preparing for birth or are being born.

Death and birth come to eternity systems, as death and birth come to man. This is the law of the greater eternal alternates, through which God circulates and animates His Spirit.

God, using the greater alternates and His Equation, created this earth or eternity system. The ancient philosophers who spoke of the cosmic musics of the universe had opened their ears to the creative tones of God's Equation.

Through communion with the cosmos, one becomes aware of man's eternal origin. He sees the universe and all eternity systems as being under the command of the Supreme Eternal Spirit,

God—and he knows eternal being is endless, ceaseless.

To think with aeon-thoughts is to know God. To accept His Plan is to move beyond day-by-day trials of endurance and frustration. All men must eventually unite with their eternal natures. When one decides to order his personal domain to cosmic and cosmos timing, he begins an upward climb toward God.

Those who have aeon-vision and memory see the entry of man into the earth as a joyous response to the Will of God. God, with His mighty Will, directed man's cosmos and cosmic transition into a new and wondrous birth.

Every man has something of the eternal in his soul through which he may unite with the memory of cosmos and cosmic birth. Cosmos birth occurs when one moves from one cosmic eternity system to another. As a babe in the mother's womb feels more secure when its embryonic ear lies close to the mother's heart, so does a soul in transit between eternities joyfully hasten to come close to God's heart within the cosmic womb of a new eternity.

God is Spirit. His Spirit animates all eternity systems in cosmos. His Spirit pulsates all forms in all eternities. A soul is a pulsating portion of God's Spirit.

The soul is spiritually aware of cosmos transition—and agrees to transition. It is also aware of Eternal Mediators assisting the cross-over from one eternity to another. The soul retains forever the memory of this Mediation as a joy, a courage, and a worth. Through this eternal memory, the soul knows itself to be incorruptible and eternal.

Men who rail against their existence—often saying they did not choose to be born—have little understanding of their souls and of God's intent for them. Before entering the earth, all men agreed in their souls to enter this eternity system and to master its alternating rhythms. The covenant to be born into this world or eternity system was entered into by the soul with full cognizance. Each soul in the earth agreed to work with the alternating actions in this eternity system, that the soul might gain an extended imaging power and attain greater powers of manifestation and de-manifestation.

The substance of the earth is undying and eternal—and is used over and over in and through the Will of God. All souls entered the earth that they might work within the laws of God and within His plan for man's evolvement. The purpose of this earth is to create a certain type of man with a quality of consciousness that may be attained only through initiatory processes in creation.

All eternity systems within the greater universe represent varied stages of evolvement and consciousness. Man comes to this earth or eternity system to make the effort to perfect a unique type of consciousness. He is using the tool of speech, that it may become the creative word. He is using the power of thought, that it may become the power of imaging through thought. If man fulfills his potential on earth, he will produce creative works and skills of cosmos proportion.

Transition in cosmos is a reality. Only through the study of the soul shall men be led by the golden cord of the eternal memory to the thresholds of this knowledge. However, science, within the next three hundred years, will discern, discover, and acknowledge a mighty Equation working between voids and eternity systems. They will confirm that old eternity systems assist in the creation of new eternity systems, and they will come closer to the knowledge that life is transmitted from one eternity system to another.

Cosmic birth begins when one enters a new eternity system. All souls retain the essence of the knowledge they have acquired in other eternity systems. This assists them to be born to the new eternity, but they also must yield themselves up to the helps of the mighty Beings governing the new eternity system. In the beginning of this eternity, these godly Mediators worked to form and shape man, that he might enter this earth with faculties which would insure his physical and spiritual survival.

Men look into the Milky Way and think of it mystically in their hearts; they feel an indefinable affiinity with these far-off galaxies—moving, swirling, spiraling, and dying. As science widens its sphere of action in cosmic exploration, men will learn more of the cosmos. They will become aware of eternity systems assisting other eternity systems to come to birth. They will also become aware of hostile eternity systems which assist in the death or ending of an eternity system. The scriptural statements of the world's end are rooted in fact.

God prepares a new eternity system for birth by using the *Alpha-tones* of His Equation. He also uses the combined tones of Hierarchy who work as creative Mediators for Him. The tones of Hierarchy, centered in adjacent eternity systems, unite with the Will of God that a new earth may be born.

When an eternity system is preparing for new birth, and the Alpha-tones of God sound—calling souls in other eternity systems to the new eternity—those who are to be born in the new eternity enter into a cosmos swoon. The preservation instinct which compels them to cling to their life in the eternity system they are leaving is nullified. The faculties used become static; the higher essence of these faculties is retained in the soul's record and will be utilized in the coming eternity system. The consciousness enters into a state of cosmos sleep. The vehicles or bodies not adaptable to the coming eternity system undergo a slow process of de-manifestation. However, the record of these vehicles or bodies is preserved in the memory of the soul. In the next eternity system, this record will enable the Father of the coming eternity to re-animate and shape the forms, bodies or vehicles to be used.

In the preparation for the new eternity, the soul is assisted by mighty Beings and Angels having the power of de-manifestation. These Beings and Angels assist the soul to surrender its existence in the eternity system which had been its homeplace. The soul undergoes a cosmic death, that it may have a cosmic birth in a new eternity system.

There are countless eternity systems within the greater universe or cosmos. The sun, earth, moon, and planets make up one eternity system. In this earth or eternity system, man moves from one life to another. In the eternal plan, he moves from one eternity system to another.

Before man reaches his eternal stature, he will be born innumerable times in other eternity systems. However, no one moves from one eternity system to another until the eternity system in which he finds himself has been concluded. The only time one travels from one eternity system to another is when he is born to a new eternity.

Men are ever being shaped, molded and formed by the Father and Hierarchy. The eye of our Father in Heaven will continue to envision and image men, and the benign rays of Hierarchy will persist in their shaping and forming until men become like Them. "Let us make man in our image, after our likeness." (Genesis 1:26)

Men are imaged in the Father's likeness and in Elohim-Hierarchy's likeness. Everything that Hierarchy is and everything that the Father is, men will become in eternal time. To accomplish this, they must first become like the Son of the Father—Jesus. Jesus is also the Son of man, or the Son of humankind. He is the Saviour and the Restorer of the souls of men. He came to enable men to become more than their physical natures. Jesus came to lift men of the earth, and to help them give birth to the human spirit. He came to revitalize the soul-memory in man; a memory of man's eternal nature; a memory of innumerable sojourns in other eternities. Jesus is the door through which men return to the Father and are initiated into the Christ Spirit.

The Life-tones of the Father will continue to restore the bodies of men until men have concluded their souls' work in the earth. With the coming of Jesus, the Christ Light-tones began for this eternity. When the Christ Light-tones penetrated the earth system, there began a co-alescing between the Life-tones of the Father, the prototypal tones of Hierarchy, and the Light-tones of the Christ. When the Life-tones, the prototypal tones and the Light-tones con-verged, man began his long upward climb to-ward a perfected mentality. As the Light-tones of the Christ continue to move upon men, men will become more and more noble in their thoughts, and their minds will become vortices of creation.

The Will and Law of God maintain a law of order in the life of man; this same Law times to man his self-discovery. As a wise parent places into the hands of his child an instructive object through which the child may learn, so do the Father and the greater host or Hierarchs open to man the vistas of the world and the vistas of his own nature.

The majority of man's sins are forgivable be-cause they are often caused by cosmic agitation and by little-known frequencies of which man is unaware—as he does not yet have the mentality or the understanding to cope with them.

Much of that which is unstable in the emo-tions of man is caused by unharnessed cosmic energy. For everything which man masters, there awaits him the mastering of billions of other influences of cosmic energy.

The energies of the elements and the atmospheres—and the unrefined electrical and magnetic frequencies creating pressure upon man— exert unrelenting pressures upon his bodies, emotions, and mind. Man has yet to discover and to utilize the energies of the sun, of the planets, and of other eternity systems—energies which enter into the atmosphere of the earth.

There is a mercy providence protecting man's unknowing. In his evolvement, man receives this providence through the help of the angels who assist him to survive calamities caused by external pressures and conditions he little understands.

Science will prove that there is an intelligible plan in earth systems. Science will admit there is a supreme Intelligible Will directing the universe.

Man's evolvement is determined by his faith. Science will give a new kind of faith to man. This faith will in no way deny Jesus as the Saviour, or the story of creation in the Book of Genesis. This faith will disclose more clearly what the Bible is saying through its prophets, its seers, and its Recording Angels.

The scientific age now places upon man multiple pressures which coincide with multiplicity gifts from the soul.

As men turn to the Jesus Ethic, they will incorporate an enlarged radius of action into their characters, temperaments, and spiritual proclivities.

The new cultures to come will demand more of man in creation. They will set new mental and ethical standards in society—and man will respond to the rising tide of creation.

Men are now on trial to die to their barbaric and atavistic wills. A world initiation sets up a mist in which men fail to see the spiritual countenances of their fellow men; they also fail to hear what is being said. However, they respond when soul-urgency fuses with mankind's emergency.

Man is a builder in the earth. He is in a continual state of building new bodies, of experiencing unfamiliar feelings, and of coming to grips with thoughts emanating from his own soul and from the souls of other men. Even as men continually renew their cells and their blood, so do they work without ceasing to incorporate new vitalities into their emotions and thoughts.

God has given man eternal time. This cosmic eternity is a system of gradation supported by gradual processes of evolution and evolvement. God does not expect of His children more than they can do. He sent His Son to assist them in the latter phases of the Alpha-tones, that they might produce the epitome of creation within themselves, and thus be prepared for the *Ome-*

ga-tones to produce a more equitable harmony within their spirits.

Men must assist one another. They also must love one another. Only through love may they fulfill the Plan of God in totality.

A man without compassion is a humanless man. A man with soul-insight sees into his brother's heart and assists him. Inasmuch as he knows himself to be yet imperfect, he does not expect his brother, his neighbor, his child, or his mate to be perfect.

Jesus knew that men were yet unformed. He knew the face of evil. He spoke of it. He spoke of the world's ending. He also spoke of the outer rim of darkness and the gnashing of teeth. He came to give formulas for life, for healing, for penetration into Heaven. He also came to show men that the earth is a threshing floor of initiation where men are shaped and molded and formed through the assistance of the angels and the power of heavenly Mediation.

Jesus based His total works for man upon His knowing of the direct procedures of Mediation. However, He promised nothing if a person placed his faith in imperfect sources of mediation. He came to call men to a noble life and to show them how to sustain their capacities and how to excel in their potentials.

Jesus had remembrance of all things—heavenly and eternal. He spoke with authority into

the ear of him who had an ear to hear. He taught
men how to pray, that they might return to the
naive androgynous state of the soul.

The etheric body of Jesus is now the etheric
body of this earth. When men observe a holy
agape, they eat of His body. When men pray,
He prays with them to the Father. When men
give form to the statements of Jesus and live
within His Ethic—and become healers and
manifestors—they are in Him, as He is in the
Father; the Father then becomes real to men as
the Imager of their being.

Jesus had known the Father throughout many
eternity systems. He and the Father were *co-
atom* to one another. Jesus entered this eternity
system with the Father. The Father had taught
Him and had instructed Him orally, as from one
Being to another. Therefore, He could say with
authority that the Father had told Him what
to say. He could also state that He was one
with the Father and that the Father was in
Him. When the earth is concluded, Jesus will
be the reigning Hierarch of this eternity
system.

The Christ Spirit is the only begotten Son of
God. As God is Eternal Spirit, the Christ is Divine Spirit. God, Eternal Spirit, is in all Beings,
persons, animals. His Spirit is also in inorganic
matter and in the plant kingdom. God wills an
eternity system to begin. The Christ Spirit works

as Mind. The Christ Spirit is in command of the greater archetypes of Mind.

When Jesus was ready for His human-spirit sovereignty, the Christ Spirit filled Him. Jesus took a physical body when men had reached the heaviest point of sentient and gravity action, that He might lift them, heal them, and teach them of the eternals, and also make them aware of our Father which art in Heaven.

Father, I will that they also, whom thou hast given me, be with me where I am; that they may behold my glory, which thou hast given me; for thou lovedst me before the foundation of the world.

—St. John 17:24

3

BIRTH OF THE EARTH

The music of God comes not to the clamorous mind. The music of God can be heard only within the still waters of the spirit.

The music of God has sent forth His universe, His galaxies, His stars. All eternity systems are the children of stars which have resounded through many eternal days in incessant creation, obedient to God.

The Spirit of God is the Word. The combined tones of His Word are perpetually and eternally shaping and forming under the direction of His Will.

COSMOS ATOMS

The universe or greater cosmos is a mighty sea of tone, light, atoms, ether, and energy. God's total universe is a vast threshing floor in which central suns or stars are born and die.

In greater cosmos, there are uncountable *cosmos atoms* swimming in a universal sea of ether and light. All cosmos atoms are potential suns. Some cosmos atoms are in a state of interim quiescence or creative rest; these cosmos atoms await eternal quickening tones, or Alpha-tones, that they may begin to manifest new eternity systems. Other cosmos atoms, receiving Omega-tones, move with a more ponderous velocity, as they are in the process of a de-manifesting action; these are dying eternity systems.

When a new eternity is to be born, God sounds Omega or dissonant, de-manifesting tones upon one or more dying eternity systems—so that the souls ready for transition to the new eternity may be released. God, using His Alpha-tones, focuses His creative Will upon a cosmos atom ripe for creation. He works simultaneously with the Omega or de-manifesting tones upon the dying eternity systems and with the Alpha-tones upon the new eternity system. This is God's Word and Equation in action.

Each cosmos atom is encased in an envelope of ether, called an *etheric encasement*. When the Alpha-tones of God begin to sound upon the centermost point of a cosmos atom, the etheric encasement around the cosmos atom becomes a *living void*. The dormant life retained in the etheric encasement around the cosmos atom is stirred and animated.

When God establishes a new void for an eternity system, He stabilizes the etheric encasement surrounding the cosmos atom, that it may sustain the coagulating of the eternity system to be born. The cosmos atom in the center of the etheric encasement becomes as the heartbeat of God. God's pulsating Will, Life, Light, and Love, sounding within the cosmos atom, summon correlated souls ready for transit into the new void or world-to-be.

During great periods of universal transition and creation, adjacent cosmos atoms become penetrable to one another. This penetration works as emanation and pulsation. When a cosmos atom is prepared to receive new life into its void, the souls being drawn into the void are immersed in a cosmic cloud of innumerable atoms. The souls and the accompanying myriad atom substances respond to the power of the cosmos atom compelling them to enter the stream of new birth.

All souls born to a new earth bring with them a cosmos dowry to give a new vitality to their future eternity home.

When the cloud of multitudinous atoms moves into the void of an earth-to-be, this sets up a new response from the existing life contained within the etheric encasement of the cosmos atom. From this combination of old eternity and new eternity, new forms of organisms and bacteria begin.

The cosmos atom generating a new eternity contains a basic or primary foundation for germinal life. This remnant of living and germinal substances is quickened and utilized when the Alpha-tones sound for the beginning of a new eternity. The incoming life from the dying eternities adds other atom vitalities to these substances—thereby producing new forms and activities.

As souls move from one eternity system to another, they move on Light-beams set up between the cosmos atom centered in the new system and the cosmos atoms of the eternity systems from which they are departing.

Scientific research into the atoms of the physical world will gradually come to reveal that the centermost part of the sun began as a mighty eternal atom, or cosmos atom. Such cosmos atoms are the motivating generators of all eternity systems.

Each eternity system in God's universe begins as a void generated by a central cosmos atom. This cosmos atom explodes and becomes a sun. In an eternity system supporting sentient life, the first explosion is followed by a sequence of other explosions which eject an earth and its accompanying planets.

WORLD-SOUL ATOM

When the cosmos atom centered in the starry body of the sun set free the earth, a mighty *world-soul atom* was quickened within the forming mass of the earth. The world-soul atom of the earth became the bride, and the cosmos atom became the bridegroom. God directed His Alpha-tones to the cosmos atom in the sun and the world-soul atom in the forming earth. Masses or bodies of molten matter were subsequently ejected from the earth. As each portion of flaming matter left the earth, an axis-atom was quickened in the center of the mass. These flaming masses became the planets accompanying the sun, the moon, and the earth. Each planet began to sound an individual tone which would respond for aeons of time to the earth's tone, the moon's tone, the sun's cosmos-atom tone, and to the axis-atom tones in sister and brother planets. The sun, the earth, the moon, and the planets began their eternity sojourn; moving together in a cosmic harmony; responding, humming and surging with the earth's creation—preparing for the coming forth of man.

In each eternity system where consciousness and sentient life are to be experienced, a world-soul atom takes command over one particularized planet or earth. Only in an earth containing consciousness life may there be found a world-soul atom. The planets accompanying an earth and a sun are but contributory factors or supplementary bodies enabling the earth to be fortified by certain energies, certain rhythms and tides of the cosmic activity.

The reach of the world-soul atom encases the moon, the planets, and the sun. Thus the earth becomes the wife of the sun; the planets, children of the sun; the moon, the discarded placenta of the earth.

The world-soul atom extends its influence into the planets and the sun. This makes it possible for the eternity system to move in its orbital and correlated life.

The cosmos atom in the sun never ceases to control the world-soul atom centered in the core of the earth. The cosmos atom, working with the world-soul atom, transmits to the earth the archetypal and generation prototypal impulses of Hierarchy and the Father. When this occurs, the sun has found its rhythm; the earth its polarity; and the planets become bodies of mediation and unison suitable for stimulating the primary mineral and atmospheric substances and elements for life on earth. The Species Angels overdwelling the animal kingdom stir the generation archetypes of the animals to take form in the earth. The Terrestrial Angels, working with the Flora Angels, revitalize the flora archetypes to quicken the plants and foliage of the earth. The generation archetypes sound the tone of life in man; the etheric form of man is then clothed in a physical body; the glands and arteries are simultaneously ripened through the pressures of gravity.

When men entered this earth system, they were first etheric. When they fell into gravity, due to solidification of the earth, their first skin covering was cork-like—with an enlarged porous texture. Their lungs were unable to take the total burden of breathing the raw gravity atmosphere; therefore, the enlarged pores of their skin enabled them to master the fume-like atmosphere. As the atmosphere cleared, the lungs became sufficient instruments for inhaling and exhaling. The blood of the human body became a finer substance, gas-like, through which cells of the physical body might be regenerated and rejuvenated.

The etheric content in the blood of man still contains something of the primitive memory of these beginning aeons. From the blood, man may read the pictures of his earth generation, of his ancestral generation, and of his individual generation.

As matter was gradually mastered, the texture of man's skin became finer. As men move toward the ending of this eternity system, their skins will become translucent and radiant—similar to the shining face of Moses when he was illumined, and to the transfiguring light of Jesus when He was transfigured. Men's blood streams, being filled with emanations from higher degrees of thought and emotions, will contain less mineral fire and more etheric fire. Thus, as men evolve in this earth, their skins will become finer and finer, until they may be said to appear like the Lord Jesus in transfigured light.

ETERNAL SUSTAINING ATOM

Each thing in the earth, from plant to man, has an *eternal sustaining atom*. Each eternal sustaining atom has a degree of light correlating to the Will, Life, Light, and Love of God. The degree of light within an eternal sustaining atom determines the form it will manifest and express, and also determines what it will contribute to the universal plan.

The eternal sustaining atom sustains life eternal from one eternity to another. The eternal sustaining atom is the means through which one moves from one eternity to another. When one prepares to enter into a new eternity or the beginning of a new eternity, his soul and the atoms for his future bodies are encased etherically within the eternal sustaining atom. Even as a person is unaware of his encasement within the womb of his mother, so was he unaware of his eternal sustaining atom encasement when he entered this eternity. The eternal sustaining atom works with God's creative fiat, and adapts itself to the eternity in which it finds itself.

The sun, the earth, and the accompanying planets are part of a network of *eternal verte-*

brae consisting of eleven other eternity systems. When these eleven sister and brother eternity systems reach a certain balance in their equation, they merge their tones with the Alpha-tones as sent forth from God. These tones become mighty transmitting streams of energy and light through which the various eternal sustaining atoms containing the forms of life-to-be are transported into the void of this eternity system.

In the beginning of this eternity the Elohim-Hierarchy, dwelling within adjacent eternity systems, and our Father of this eternity sounded Life-tones into the world-soul atom. Their combined Life-tones played upon the innumerable eternal sustaining atoms dwelling in the cosmic mist of the yet unformed earth.

In the first Edenic or etheric intervals of the earth's creation, the Father of this eternity— working with the Elohim-Hierarchy, the Archangels, Angels, and other Presences—imaged all things as they were to be formed in this eternity. The Father, using the Life-Fiat, animated the original blueprints or archetypes of all living things to come.

The eternal sustaining atom is the supreme atom of the eternal atoms of man. When men were first immersed and encased in this eternity system, their eternal or spiritual atoms—containing aeonic intelligence—began their responding immediately to the cosmic pre-natal helps given by Hierarchy, our Father, the Christ, and the Archangels.

All that the soul has experienced in former eternities, all that has been earned, is encapsuled and retained in the eternal sustaining atom.

Light is the very essence of man's eternal being. Each soul on earth attained certain degrees of light while living in other eternity systems before this earth or eternity system was ever created. The degrees of light one attained in former eternities are sustained eternally in the eternal sustaining atom; they are never lost. The eternal degrees of light work in unison with the pulsation of the soul.

When the soul enters a new eternity system, the cosmos atom of the new eternity quickens the soul's pulsation within the eternal sustaining atom. Within each eternal sustaining atom there is also a cosmos pulsation enabling man to work with the greater alternates of cosmos, and to respond to the eternal laws. The creative side of the *cosmos alternates* is used by Hierarchy, the Archangels, the Christ, and the Father to shape and form men.

There are also *cosmic alternates* affecting men. These assure men of night and day, of cold and heat, of time, cycles, and seasons, and of the incoming and outgoing tides of the oceans and waters of the earth.

There are also *gravity alternates*. These pertain to the magnetic and the electrical currents of the earth. The gravity alternates enable man to use an upright spine. They enable him to use the contraction and expansion of his lungs, the voluntary and involuntary nervous and muscular systems of the physical body. The gravity alternates enable the heartbeat to maintain the balance within the pulse points of the body.

The Satanic or Luciferic Angels work to draw men downward to the lower side of the gravity alternates, and thus bring temptation and destruction to men. Satan or Lucifer and his dark angels work upon the will of man. They seek to immobilize man's loving emotions. They also use the lower electrical, gravity alternates to subtly inject doubt and depression into the thoughts of man. These fallen angels were cast out of Heaven by the Father. The power of Heaven is greater than the power of Satan. If a man consents to come under Satan, he invites destruction.

The eternal sustaining atom enables the soul to work with two polarities. This causes a duality action of positive and negative in the emotions, thoughts, conscience, and actions of man. This duality action also enables one to take either a masculine or feminine form, and provides the way through which one may work in the physical gravity world and still remain communicable to the Heaven Worlds. The eternal sustaining atom will make it possible eventually for man to give birth to a third or triplicity polarity action; this will produce an androgynous will and mentality.

In this eternity, the eternal sustaining atom is at home within the archetypes of the Kingdom of God. When one uses the multiplicity power of his spiritual atoms, the eternal sustaining atom and its eternal action will be disclosed to him. And there will no longer be any doubt as to eternal life and eternal being.

4

THE BODIES OF MAN

This is the measure of the days: Man must make the human spirit more majestic, that the soul of the human spirit may shine. The human spirit would speak through the souls of all men, and lift men above the raucous and infantile, that they might come into human dignity and maturity.

The human spirit and the Eternal One work in man, that man may perfect the earth, using the essences of the earth and the essences within himself. The Life Spirit, which has established itself in man throughout the eternities and the ages, now gives more vigor to the human spirit, that man may become more than an echo of his Lord.

When men defile the human spirit, they defeat the Plan of the Eternal One. When the human spirit is fulfilled, man will use Life Spirit reverently; he will become a pro-genesis man. He will stand in the Father's work, and will be even as the Lord Jesus—at one with the Father.

The soul must be free to give range to its work in the two worlds—Heaven and earth. Therefore, in this eternity the soul required more than one body, that it might experience the perpetual interchange set up by the cause and effect existing between Heaven and earth. There are periods when the soul chooses to inhabit lighter bodies, that it may refresh itself in heavenly atmospheres; and there are periods when the soul by necessity chooses to take bodies more cumbersome, that it may be armored against elements, frictions, tensions.

Our eternity system is but one among billions of other eternity systems. On entering this eternity, men first lived in an etheric state; they responded to the voice of God. Some remembered whence they came. Gradually, as the earth began to shape and form, etheric man was compelled to cope with the gravity action within a more dense atmosphere. An emotional, mental, physical, and lesser etheric body were formed. The soul-faculties were confronted with a new world, through which the Spirit of God might create and expand.

Over the aeons and ages men moved away from their eternal memory and became more physical. The cosmos-eternal man remembers his eternal beginnings, and he lives to remind other men that there is a third aspect in their being which can only be manifested through the love of God, love of life, and love of one's fellow man. This third aspect is a godly love beyond the alternates of love and hate commonly known to man.

The eternal sustaining atom enables a soul to travel from eternity to eternity. After the eternal sustaining atom has come to rest in a new eternity, the exalted Presences of Mediation direct their imaging tones upon the eternal sustaining atoms. The Father, the Christ, Hierarchy, and the Archangels assist those to be born to the new world to produce bodies equal to the pressures and necessities of forthcoming existences and life. Slowly, the atoms encased in the eternal sustaining atom press forth into the etheric atmospheric light; and gradually, over an extended period, the soul and the eternal sustaining atom project the etheric mold for the bodies necessary for life on earth and in Heaven.

In birth to this eternity it was necessary for the soul to have suitable vehicles or bodies for this eternity; it was also vital that the soul retain a body of spiritual light with which to experience Heaven.

When God created this eternity—and centered His pulsating Will, Life, Light, and Love within the cosmos atom sustaining the new eternity—He gave to men a Heaven and an earth. He called upon Elohim-Hierarchy and the Father to become the Over-Lords and Gov-

ernors of Heaven and earth. He called upon the
Christ Spirit to establish the greater archetypes
and blueprints to be activated in the world. He
called upon the Archangels to reign over all
other angels—the Celestial Angels, Recording
Angels, Guardian Angels, Procreation Angels,
Seraphim, Cherubim, and Terrestrial Angels.
He assigned to each soul a Recording Angel, a
Guardian Angel, an angel for the mind (Niscience Angel), an angel for the emotions (Angel
of Pure Desiring), and an angel for the physical
body (Luminosity Angel).

In an eternity system creating through the
greater alternates, souls are provided with a
physical body containing the life substance of
blood; an emotional body through which they
may feel and love; a mental body with which
to reason, to judge, and to think; a lesser etheric
body through which they may regenerate and
revitalize their life energies, and through which
they may assist Nature in consuming the physical body at death. A higher etheric body, or
everlasting body, is also given to each soul, providing man with the ability to transcend the
lower side of the alternate of pain or the destroying principle.

Through the light of his soul, the higher
degrees of light in his mind, and the higher
degrees of light in his emotions, man uses his
eternal heritage to overcome weaknesses and

negations. In his heavenly body, or everlasting body, man is "like" the angels; he communes with the angels; he receives their ministering strengths and helps through his heavenly body.

In his mental body, man is able to be telepathically aligned with the thoughts of other men. When the mental body is at one with the soul's light, one communes with the greater ideas of God, and has access to the imaging aspect of our Father which art in Heaven.

The emotional body enables man to love the Lord of Love; to love God's Heaven; to commune with God through love. Through his love for God, he loves his fellow man.

The physical body enables man to function within the pressures of gravity that he may become a steward of the chemicals, minerals, plants, and animals of the earth. In his physical body he is able to travel throughout the earth, to cultivate its soil, to build cities, industry, bridges. He is able to use the generation impulses of his body to provide physical bodies for souls entering the physical world.

The lesser etheric body is a solar sentinel in the day, energizing the blood stream of the physical body; maintaining circulation of the blood; generating vitality and well-being; and keeping a balance between energies of light and energies of gravity. At night, the lesser etheric body is a lunar sentinel, watching over man's physical body during sleeping hours while he moves in his higher bodies into heavenly initiatory precincts, and communes with the Holy Presences.

The physical body, the lesser etheric body, and the lesser emotional body are perishable bodies. The higher emotional body, the higher aspects of the mental body, and the higher etheric body or everlasting body are eternal and incorruptible.

The physical and lesser etheric bodies of man can combat the elements, the energies, and the tensions just so long in the physical world. Through continued erosions and pressures, the physical body yields gradually to the destroying principle—and death ensues. However, the higher emotional body, the higher aspects of the mental body, and the higher etheric body are the incorruptible bodies of man. They know not death; they live eternally. They are eternal because they have functioned before in this eternity, and in other eternities.

In each eternity system, God draws upon the substances supporting the eternity to provide bodies for the souls inhabiting that eternity. When this eternity system was created, man was given a physical body made up of the substances of the earth. The bodies used by man, animals and creatures were drawn or extracted from the earth's substances.

All substances of the earth consist of light.

Inorganic and organic matter function in slower degrees of light. The physical body is a body of earth-light. The emotional body is a body of electro-magnetic light. The mental body is a body of electrical light. The lesser etheric body is a body of solar and lunar light. The everlasting body, or higher etheric body, is a body of spiritual light.

In the early Edenic life, man's everlasting body, or higher etheric body, was the first body manifested. As the spiritual light became more and more intense within the eternal sustaining atom of man, an ovoid emotional body was formed, containing the higher emotional and sentient atoms; and a mental body, containing the mental atoms, was formed.

As the earth cooled, a lesser etheric body was produced—containing twelve vortices of light reflecting the alternating currents of Hierarchy. These alternating currents of Hierarchy in the lesser-etheric-body vortices work in clockwise and contraclockwise action. When one is negative, his lesser-etheric-body vortices move in contraclockwise action, and he receives the forceful rather than the spiritual energies of the planets. When the vortices work in a clockwise action, man experiences the higher energies of the planets, and he is inspired to look toward the spiritual rather than the depressive side of the emotions. By remaining constant to the spir-

itual life, and observing a constant holy reverence, one keeps the vortices of the lesser etheric
body in clockwise motion.

After the higher etheric and emotional bodies
were manifested, a mental body was formed,
having three active atoms and nine dormant
atoms. The three mental atoms enabled man to
experience memory, to will, and to image. It
will be impossible for man to image as a Hierarch until he has quickened the nine remaining
mental atoms of his mental body. It will be impossible for him to will as the Hierarchs or
exalted Presences until he has activated all
mental body atoms.

The physical body has nine activated atoms
which correlate to the nine orifices in man's
physical body. As man becomes a perfected
being in the earth, the three remaining atoms
of the physical body will be activated in three
polarity points in his body: one in the gonad
area, which will enable him to use the procreative power sacredly; the second in the heart
area, which will place the organ of the heart in
the center of his body. The heart will develop
an additional muscle power, enabling man to
command the health of his body. When this
occurs, he will be without toxins, poisons or
infections. He will generate children who are
chaste and pure. His blood memory of ancestry
will enable him to draw upon his eternal ances-

try and grace ancestry rather than his sexual
ancestry. There will be no lust passions in his
blood stream. The atom of his heart will be a
generative dynamo of joyous love. He will know
a total soul-androgynous love, in which hate
cannot manifest in his mind, feelings or emotions. He will be as the mighty Presences in his
love.

The last or twelfth atom of the physical body
will be activated in the throat, in proximity to
the larynx. After the twelfth physical-body atom
of man has been activated, he will be free of
any inhibitions of the will—his will having
gained free interflow between the spinal canal
and the brain. From this he will produce a
fluidic will; a fiery canal within the spinal cord
will remain continually open. He will become
like Jesus, with the power to manifest new
vitalities and energies—and he will have the
power to de-manifest corrupt things, sicknesses
and ailments.

At present, man uses his will with perfection
only when he has complete alignment with the
Mediation of the Lord Jesus and His angels,
and with the Holy Presences working with
Him. At present, he may image new things only
through the holy Mediative helps. He also receives the help of the angels who assist him in
fulfilling his pure covenants and dedication.

When man has activated the latent atoms in

all bodies, his procreative life will be a pure and reverent one; and he will be found worthy to give birth through his body to creative souls, who will bless not only him, but the world.

Hierarchy, the Father and the Archangels, through the use of will and imaging, assisted in the making of man's bodies. Eternal man also assisted through the powers of his eternal soul. As an infant assists its mother in birth, so did the soul of man, in the beginning of this eternity system, assist the Hierarchs and the Father. In certain depths of the soul, man still retains the memory of this shaping and forming. If he will, he may return to the memory of aeon-time. Through the powers of his soul and the use of his higher mind, he may experience eternal thoughts. His soul seeks to maintain a balance between eternal thoughts and thoughts acquired in this eternity or world.

In the beginning of this eternity, Hierarchy played the creative tones of the alternates upon the emerging wills of men, so that men, when they would inhabit the physical world, could choose between good and evil, love and hate, violence and peace, truth and untruth. The Father played His Life-tones upon man-to-be, that man might animate his bodies and give life to his ideas, his progeny, and his works. The Christ Spirit—the Son of God—played His Light-tones upon man-to-be, that man might have a quickened soul, and eventually an illumined mind; and that man would, in time, thirst for the greater ideas of truth—thereby receiving direct wisdom from the archetypes. The Archangels played their tones upon man-to-be, that he might know something of the seasons and timing, and also be subjected to the greater cosmic impulses in the solstitial and equinoctial periods of the solar year.

After the Greater Beings had concluded this phase of their work, the planets, one by one, moved into their orbs or placement in this eternity system. When the planets were projected from the earth, their tones were sealed into man's consciousness. As each planet moved away from the earth-to-be, forming man received into the lower and higher octaves of the atoms of his bodies the tones of all planets to which he would respond throughout the eternity system. In all lives to come, he would respond either to the lower tones of the planets or to the higher tones of the planets. If he succumbed to negation, he would receive the lower tones of the planets. If he set his thoughts on godly things, he would receive the higher tones of the planets.

The second stage of cosmic birth began when the earth established its gravitational polarities. Through glandular ripeness, man began to propagate and to populate the earth; he began to extend his senses, and to experiment with cause and effect.

In the next phase of cosmic birth, man began his battle with the elements, animals, Nature, persons, and with himself. The duality or alternating powers within him enabled him to choose the right or the wrong. When he learns to choose the true, he will enter into the greater phases of cosmic birth. He will become a *Jesus man,* or "like Him." (1 John 3:2)

Spiritual power is eternal power. Only through spiritual power may man master the alternates, and thereby gain a prescient consciousness. Through spiritual power, he is victor over failures and defeats. His soul, which has afforded him the opportunity to receive knowledge in many eternity systems, will remain a persistent watcher or supervisor over his works and his ways. If he errs, he will suffer—until he turns his faith to eternal verities.

Regardless of how one falls, he will arise in some time. If he has fallen too far, God in His Will and His mercy will see that he, in some eternal time, may renew himself through rebirth. In places, eternities, or mansions afar, he will be born again and start his upward climb.

Until the coming of Jesus, men lived close to their primitive survival attributes. Jesus came that men might become aware of their eternal natures. Men will be born over and over to the physical world until they have perfected their mental, emotional, and physical bodies.

When God gave man his first body in this earth—the higher etheric body—it was a perfect body. This perfect body still exists, for it is eternal. All other bodies which man has projected throughout the billions of years are yet imperfect; while functional, they are still subjected to tumults and pressures.

When men accept the fact that they live in an eternity system offering alternate action, and when they know there is a third action beyond the alternates, they will free their souls to work with the higher etheric body. Their souls will take command of the higher side of their minds, and of the higher side of their emotions. They will sculp and shape their lesser bodies through the mediation helps of Hierarchy, the Father, and the angels. Their minds will agree to accept the initiations which the soul offers through their bodies, emotions, and thoughts.

The earth is man's crucible. When man has incorporated into his mental body all of the creative ideas he has gained while mastering the physical world; when his emotional body has been perfected, and his heart has become equal to the heart of the Son of Man; when he has acquired the power of resurrection over death—his cosmic birth will be concluded, and he will begin a hierarchy work within this eternity system.

When this earth is concluded, the mind of man will have incorporated all of the substances of the earth. His soul will have regenerated the physical into spiritual, creative substances. The mental power of man will have produced a consciousness heretofore unknown to the soul.

THE MEEK AND THE END OF THE WORLD

In the Beatitudes, where Jesus states, "The meek shall inherit the earth," He was speaking of cosmos reality. Jesus, the Lord of Love, knew the earth's origin, for He had the eternal memory. Jesus remembered having lived in other eternity systems. He knew that the meek in this eternity system would inherit its post-mortem void. The meek, using mental hierarchy powers, will assist the souls leaving this eternity to respond to the Alpha-tones in the eternity where they will have their coming birth. The meek will also assist incoming souls to enter into the beginning of the new life-rhythms in the newly forming earth.

As an eternity system concludes, the sentient fire within the atoms supporting inorganic, organic, and bacterial life generates intense velocities of energy. The gravity atoms of man—supporting his physical body, his cells, and his blood system—enter into high degrees or frequencies, becoming a form of accelerated vital fire. The eternal atoms supporting his mental and emotional bodies, the pulsation of his soul, his eternal sustaining atom, and the atoms of his higher etheric body are freed from gravity action. The lower mind and lower emotions which have colored his thoughts are anesthetized. His higher emotions and thoughts, completely in accord with his soul's pulsation, make him aware of the Omega-tones and the dying of the eternity system.

If a soul has become one of the meek, he will prepare to "inhabit the earth"; he will be one of the "last" to enter into a cosmos swoon. He will remain in the etheric encasement of the eternity system, and he will be one of the "first" to receive consciousness in the next Alpha day. He will use his power of meekness and love as a co-atom creator with Hierarchy—and he will remember he has lived in the previous earth system.

The Omega-tones begin to sound when the Alpha-tones have fulfilled the Father's command in the eternity system. In this eternity system, the Alpha-tones will resound upon man until he has reached a cosmos-genesis time. Cosmos-genesis man will be a man of love, of honor, of ethic.

When the Omega-tones begin their sounding, an eternity system enters into a prolonged process of mortal death, covering billions of years. In this Omega period, man begins to usurp the powers of Nature. Nature gradually loses its compulsion to survive, and slowly retreats from man. Man depends more and more on his mentality, rather than on Nature. Highly evolved souls become increasingly aware of spiritual things and of the Spiritual Worlds.

When an eternity system's central sun prepares to die, or to end, the cosmos atom centered within the sun sends forth to the earth and the planets a tone of dissonance, or a death tone. The earth and the planets accompanying the sun begin their preparation to be drawn back into the sun. The axis-atoms within the cores of the moon and the planets slow down—and the planetary system accompanying the sun moves more ponderously. The world-soul atom within the earth, wherein the consciousness life has been expressed, begins to revolve in an eccentric manner. The earth begins to disengage itself from the magnetic gravity pull working between the moon, the sun, and the earth—and gravity becomes a strong charge of electricity.

The cosmos atom within the sun—commanding the axis-atom within each planet and the world-soul atom of the earth—uses the Omega-tones to change the orbital rhythms between the planets and the earth. The result is that the rotation of the planets and the earth around the sun is disoriented. The former orbital resiliency within the eternity system reverses, and the dying planets are compelled to return to the sun which gave them birth.

Gradually, by degrees, the cosmos atom in the sun draws the planets and earth closer and closer to the sun. As the earth and the planets come closer and closer to the sun, the atoms sustaining all forms of inorganic, plant and animal life slow down their energies. The mineral life, the sentient life, and the consciousness life in the earth of an eternity system undergo a fiery transition. The central fiery core in each planet and in the earth manifests an interior volcanic action. Over a long interval covering billions of years, the fiery core within each planet becomes an unleashed molten fiery mass, which engulfs the total planet. The earth and the planets become liquid, cup-like, floating vortices of flame. Finally, they make the shores of the sun, and are gathered into the bosom of the sun.

Slowly, over inestimable time, the fiery mass —including the sun, the planets, and the earth— cools. The remaining substances become vapor-like, and once again all that remains is an etheric encasement around the cosmos atom.

When an earth system dies, the cosmos atom and the world-soul atom merge and become as one. The world-soul atom remains within the etheric encasement, obedient to the cosmos atom which sent it forth. The etheric mold of the earth merges with the cosmos atom and world-

soul atom within the dying sun. The etheric
molds of the planets station themselves around
the earth's etheric mold or sphere.

After the world-soul atom and the cosmos
atom have completed their reconciliation, they
remain united, awaiting the next phase of their
coordinating creation. The souls awaiting transition prepare to be called to coming voids or
new eternities.

When an earth system dies, the atoms supporting the lower forms of energy separate
themselves from the higher atoms generating
spiritual light. All conscious beings are free to
live in their bodies of light, and are more aware
of the etheric energies and the higher degrees
of light affecting consciousness. Laggard souls
who have refused to keep pace in evolvement
prepare to be reborn in eternities providing
them with the degree of initiation and evolvement necessary for their souls. They will enter
into eternity systems having slower degrees of
evolvement. Those who have attained the higher
geneses will remain in the spiritual light of the
etheric encasement which surrounds the cosmos
atom, until God's Equation calls them to a new
eternity, where they will begin their next phase
of evolvement.

The meek will remain in the etheric mold of
the earth in proximity to the world-soul atom;
having inherited the earth, it will be their work

to welcome the incoming souls from other eternity systems in the next Alpha-tone day.

Assisting the meek will be the great host of angels who will also remain within the etheric encasement of the cosmos atom. These angels will resume their work in the next eternity activity.

The animals remaining in the earth will go forth with the Omega-tide to inhabit other eternity systems. At the end of this eternity, the lion and the lamb will have made peace with one another. All beasts of the field or domestic animals serving man will go forth to peaceful eternity systems where their labors will be required.

Carnivorous animals will move forth upon the Omega cosmos tide to find themselves in eternity systems where laggard souls will dwell.

In the next Alpha-day of this eternity system, a higher order of beings will inhabit the earth. There will be no animal or bird life. There will be only angelic life and man.

When the Omega-tones are concluded and all transient souls have made their exit, the cosmos atom begins to sound an eternal hum. Germinating life and consciousness life within the etheric encasement—to be used in the next phase of the eternity system—enter into an eternal hush. The cosmos atom sounds a neuter hum, and remains quiescent until God's Equation times its quickening through the mighty Alpha-tones.

5

TRIBES AND RACES

Those who sat in the Upper Chamber
with their Lord
changed their arc of genesis.
So will all men change their arc of genesis,
and rise;
for from the Christ is the rise of the arc.
And in right timing
comes the genesis
which overcomes the long, wandering way.
The accelerated timing of the Christ
brings man to that time
when he may receive
the genesis memory of the ages.

Before the Alpha-tones sounded upon the cosmos atom of the present eternity system, the etheric encasement surrounding the cosmos atom had known a previous eternity system. In the etheric encasement slept the static forms of the inhabitants of the previous eternity system. These inhabitants were the animal kingdom.

The earth in its previous existence had a life of its own—plant and animal life. The Over-Lords governing this life were the Fauna Over-Lords, the Species Over-Lords, the Fertility

Over-Lords. The plant kingdom was under command of the Great Deva Angels—the Archangels of the plant kingdom. These Angels were the directing power over the Flora Angels. The Pollinating Angels watched over all creatures having wings. The Flora Angels watched over the sacred atoms in the roots of all plants. The Fertility Angels watched over the sacred atom within the genitals of animals, insuring the continuation of the species.

In the previous cosmic eternity system of our earth, there was a plant and foliage verdancy. The vegetation and plant activity of the earth had reached a state of self-preservation and survival. Animals sustained themselves through the grains and plants, and had access to the curative and therapeutic nature of plants.

After the previous eternity system experienced the Omega-tones and reached its conclusion, all animals, plants and winged creatures inhabiting the eternity entered into a suspended cosmic sleep. They remained quiescent until the etheric encasement was re-animated by the Alpha-tones of God.

In the former eternity system, during the sounding of the Omega-tones, the vegetation life was withdrawn. Some of the more aggressive animals became carnivorous and devoured the weaker species among the animals. The aggressive animals retained these carnivorous traits when this eternity system began anew. All carnivorous animals existing in the earth today are remnants of such animals.

When man began to walk the earth, carnivorous animals looked upon him as a creature of prey. The carnivorous animal was man's first encounter with fear in the beginning of the human spirit.

When men came to this eternity system, animals entered another cosmic phase in their evolution.

Man has never been an animal and will never be an animal. Those who seek to solve the origin of man through the animal kingdom are being led into error. As long as man needs the animal kingdom, the animals will serve him.

Animal will never become man, but the animal empathy which man has the grace to receive in this eternity has become a part of man's sentient nature, as well as a part of his instinctual nature.

The animals are necessary to man, even as the angels are necessary to him. Man is chameleon-like to the animal kingdom and to the angelic kingdom. He absorbs from these two kingdoms certain fortifying attributes. The animal kingdom supports him in his earth sojourn, and the angels support him in his heavenly sustaining.

It is the animals' destiny to serve men and to be companions to them. The animal kingdom, being first quickened to awareness of its mission in the earth, began to look toward the incoming life—man—who was to walk with it throughout many eternity days.

Previous to man's taking a gravity body, the animals had established the role they were to play in the life of man. Harmless animals assisted by the Species Fauna Angels joyfully prepared to welcome man, that he might receive of their noble strength and help.

Consciousness souls entering this eternity system were held in an etheric state in their forming and shaping, while the plant kingdom and the animal kingdom prepared the atmosphere of the earth for man's coming. Man remained in the etheric state until the animals and the plants had purified the gases and volcanic fumes of the earth.

The Hierarchs do not work with the plant or animal kingdom. They work only with consciousness souls. The men of this earth have consciousness souls, mentalities, and soul-faculties with sense attributes. These they had developed and used in the various eternity systems from which they had come.

The Will of God ordained that men of this eternity system be under the command of the Elohim-Hierarchy and a Supreme Hierarch—our Father which art in Heaven. The Father—under the direction of Eternal Spirit, or God—

was the first Omniscient *Being* to work with the etheric encasement surrounding the cosmos atom of this eternity system.

There is a Father in each eternity system. God, Eternal Spirit, works through the Fathers of all eternity systems. The Fathers are Omniscient Beings. God is Omnipotent Spirit.

When the first Alpha-tones were sounded upon the cosmos atom of this eternity system, the Hierarchs centered in adjacent eternity systems used their creative rays in conjunction with God's eternal Will fiat and Alpha-tones. Our Father of the earth worked directly with the Elohim-Hierarchs in the making and imaging of men.

As the earth became more solid, souls were ready for birth to the earth. The gravity pressures began to stir the senses of man. A glandular system within the cell or blood body of man came to ripeness. Countless souls were born with bodies of blood and cells. These souls were androgynous, having the male and female polarities in an equal state. However, this androgynous state was not suitable for propagating the earth; therefore, all souls who had taken gravity bodies entered into a second cosmic sleep. During this sleep, the Alpha-tones—working with Hierarchal dual tones and with the Father and His power of imaging—changed the rhythms of the androgynous action into a dual action.

". . . male and female created He them."
(Genesis 1:27) Following this, the first life-
wave of humanity souls awakened and saw
themselves to be male and female. Thus began
the separation of the sexes or the divided polarities in the world.

After the division of the sexes, the world-
soul atom quickened the moon's generation impulses. The Race Lord, called Jehovah, began
his work. This Race Lord, who worked with
the axis-tone of the moon, divided the humanity
of the earth into four races. These races are
allegorically mentioned in the Bible as the
river from Eden with "four heads." (Genesis
2:10-14).

The first race quickened by Jehovah was red.
As the earth's atmosphere fell upon the crimson
ether around the sacred atoms in the hearts of
these men, their skins took on a rosy glow.
Jehovah quickened a second race; as their sacred
atoms had certain darkened ether, their skins
became black. Following this, Jehovah stirred
another race; their sacred atoms, having an
ochre-colored ether, transposed the life energies
into yellow and brown skin colors. Lastly, Jehovah, with the help of the Father and Hierarchy,
quickened the ivory-like ether in the sacred
atoms of the fourth race. This produced a race
with lighter, milk-like skin. This nucleus of
souls had used a certain mental creativity in

former eternity systems. They became the "tall men" mentioned in the Bible. Jehovah sounded the procreation tones upon the tall men, and they entered into cohabitation with women of the red race. From this came the so-called white man of the earth.

> **There were giants in the earth in those days; and also after that, when the sons of God came in unto the daughters of men, and they bare children to them, the same became mighty men which were of old, men of renown.**
>
> **—Genesis 6:4**

The "giants" in this passage of the Old Testament relate to the greater Elect who now dwell in the Spiritual Worlds. These spiritual Beings with celestial powers were called "the sons of God" because they were conscious co-workers with Hierarchy in the beginning of the earth's creation. Such giants, or the great Elect, projected themselves into the earth after the Adam humanity had established its acts of generation or propagation. The Elect cohabited with the daughters of men and produced an Elect with a slightly lesser degree of evolvement. Their children or offspring were to become mighty men, who had been great in other eternities previous to this earth. (". . . which were of old, men of renown.") Such men were to become in future lives the great prototypal patriarchs, such as Noah, Enoch, and Abraham.

All souls of the human spirit are the same in the eyes of our Father, Hierarchy, and God. Jehovah divided men into races because they had different eternity backgrounds. Those having more quickened ether in their atoms had come from eternity systems having different velocities in creation.

When a cosmos atom responds to the Alpha-tones, God wills to what degree there shall be variety, assimilation, and also, separation. When the four races had been established, they were commanded to multiply in the earth. Race Lord Jehovah placed an etheric encasement around each race, uniting its members through racial ties and affinities. He assigned racial Guardian Angels to watch over their propagation, that they might perfect the race ideal for this eternity system. He also assigned Judgment and Recording Angels over the four races to protect the races from cohabitation with each other. The "tall men" returned to their androgynous state; their remnant or progeny became the door and the key through which men would eventually be freed of the race boundaries and divisions.

Jehovah, in command of the races, dispersed the races into nomadic tribes. They wandered the earth, following the agrarian harvest. Enmity in the earth was a rare thing in the beginning of this eternity. The first humanities had not the aggressions that men know today. They were still obedient to the voice of the Father and to the voice of Jehovah. They lived in a form of etheric knowing, fortified by earth skills.

Many of the carnivorous animals of the earth preyed upon man. Man began to domesticate other animals. He watched their habits and took on some of their self-preservation instincts. The animals led him with the seasons to green and verdant fields.

During this period of man's life on earth, he was agrarian, and obeyed completely the voice of the Father which told him to eat of the fruits and the grains. The naming power man had received from the Father enabled him to identify creature companions in the world. Man named the races; he named the animals; he named the fish; he named the feathered creatures; he named the plants of the field.

The human-spirit man of that time loved with a child-like love. He mated in a composite mating season. Children were born each year for all men at the same time. For long aeons, men lived in this semi-Eden in the earth. Then, a certain thing was developed in men's natures— in the latter days of semi-Eden, certain evil traits appeared in strong, more forceful men of the tribes. The separation between tribes became more distinct. The more forceful men began to kill some of their animal friends.

In these days of semi-Eden, there occurred great floods and tidal waves; for the tones of the cosmos atom in the sun, the world-soul atom in the earth, and the axis-atoms in the planets combined to establish separation of land into continents. When this occurred, the earth experienced a cosmic convulsion. Semi-Eden, situated in the eastern part of the earth, was shifted northward. The mountain ranges of the earth existing in semi-Eden shifted to run north and south, rather than east and west.

Semi-Eden ceased to be. Physical men who survived took command of the portion of the earth left to them. Their ancestral memory enabled them to use their tribal crafts to survive. They appointed chiefs or leaders to lead them. Each chief was selected for his power of etheric memory.

The Judgment Angels imposed retribution upon the tribe when the members of the tribe failed to obey the taboos established by their chief.

The worthy chiefs lived under the guidance of Jehovah and the Judgment Angels. They directed the tribes as to wanderings, or to the selection of sites for their villages and communal life. There was movement all over the face of the earth. Men were still wanderers. Yet as time moved on, under the direction of the chiefs, they began to use their hands and minds to build monuments and altars. The chief of the tribe taught them to worship Spirit, and to know there was a directing Spirit reigning over the tribe.

When a tribal nucleus reached a point of obedience and purity as to trait, character and strength, a laggard member of the tribe, using perverted acts of witchcraft, contested the etheric authority of the chief and cast doubt in the minds of his fellow tribesmen. When this occurred, the Guardian Angels and the Judgment Angels over the tribe would withdraw the generative life-spirit of the tribe sustaining the begetting of children—and one by one, the members of the tribe would become impotent and sterile.

During these days the chieftain would be overthrown. Men would follow the darker soul. They would fall into cannibalism, and, after a period of time, the tribe would vanish from the earth. Such souls would remain in lengthy periods of sleep in the interior worlds, to be born anew in the earth through tribes experiencing hardships, famines, cataclysms, and plagues.

When the tribes had been established, Hierarchy and our Father began to sound higher tones of generation into the archetypes overdirecting the human spirit. Each man began to be the chief of his own house. In this period, the tribal encasement began gradually to change to family-atom encasement. Man began to learn the rugged lesson of family survival, rather than the survival of tribes. No longer dependent upon the chief in a tribe, he had to rely upon his own resources for survival. He began to learn that he must choose his own mate and protect her for the sake of their children.

Before this earth is concluded, the human spirit will progress through seven geneses: (1) tribal or nomadic-genesis, (2) family or human-genesis, (3) lesser and higher self-genesis, (4) cosmos-genesis, (5) pro-genesis, (6) all-genesis, (7) one-genesis. God gave the seven geneses to man that man might perfect a certain type of mind in this eternity system. The first three geneses were given to man that he might perfect temperament, character, individuality, and soul-expression. The last four geneses were given to man that he might recover his awareness of eternal things and express a certain degree of consciousness under the direction of the Father, Hierarchy, the Christ Spirit, and the Holy Presences of Heaven.

Until the coming of Jesus, men built their bodies through their senses. All feelings and thoughts were colored by mass compulsions. With the coming of Jesus, true individuality began. When men reach pure self-genesis and come into alignment with the Christ-impulse through their soul-expression, they will bring to the world a unique consciousness. Man now enters an age of extreme pressure and self-discipline to enable him to free his senses into soul-faculties, and thus align himself with the pure ideas in the world of God.

When men are in pro-genesis, they shall be "like" Jesus.

Beloved, now are we the sons of God, and it doth not yet appear what we shall be; but we know that, when he shall appear, we shall be like him; for we shall see him as he is. And every man that hath this hope in him purifieth himself, even as he is pure.

—1 John 3:2,3

The first three geneses cover a period of billions of years. They are designed to accomplish three things:

I. Physical form—a body for action
II. Personality—a body for experience
III. Individuality—a body for thought.

Tribal-genesis is for the purpose of giving man the coordinated use of the senses, and a perfected physical form as an instrument for physical action, in preparation for the ages to come. Through wars between tribes, man begins the evolvement of an *individualistic atom* in his physical body. This individualistic atom in his physical body works with the microscopic form-image within the sacred atom of the heart, and gives him a consciousness pertaining to his physical body. It makes man aware of his physical body and what it may do for him. It makes him aware of all things having a form. It also makes it possible for the physical form to be reproduced from life to life.

In tribal or nomadic-genesis, man's ideal is preservation of the tribe. Before man used a gravity body, he used his Edenic senses or soul-faculties. In his gravity body, he began to think through the combined senses of his tribe. In tribal-genesis, until the time of Jesus, man's conscience was centered in the taboos of the tribe and was overdirected by the elders of the tribe. The Jehovah Race-Guardian Angels and Recording Angels spoke into the ears and thoughts of the elders of the tribe. From this the sexual taboos were established for the tribe. The agrarian laws were understood as to the time of sowing and reaping. The knowledge of how to utilize grains, fruits, herbs, and nuts suitable to the tribal health was received directly by the matriarchs of the tribe whose ears were open to the words of the Guardian Angel of the tribe. The women of the tribe also learned how to care for their young. They observed the animal kingdom, and understood its laws of mating and begetting.

Childbirth in tribal life was under the direction of the tribal and racial Propagation Angels. Women who lived close to the Guardian Angel of the tribe received an etheric anaesthesia during childbirth, and thus child-bearing was a painless and natural part of the rhythm of their lives.

In tribal-genesis, man reincarnated in life-waves or in masses of humanity. From life to life he alternated his sex from male to female, female to male. Men worked through a common conscience of the tribe rather than through individual conscience. The errors of the tribe were purged through cataclysms, famines, plagues, floods, wars.

The Jehovah Recording Angels inspired men within tribes to understand the forces of Nature, the Nature Spirits, and the elementals; and also directed them to virginal places to establish their tribal communities. The Jehovah Recording Angels recorded the history of the tribes and races, the history of their wars, their defeats and victories, their floods and cataclysms, their plagues, curses, and dissensions.

The Race Guardian Angels worked to sustain the courage of men in tribes and races during great floods, cataclysms, and catastrophies. The Race Guardian Angels stimulated men to migrate and worked with them during periods of migration. They inspired men to profusely propagate—and to establish the sacred taboos to protect the purity of the tribe or race. During great periods of trial, the leaders of the races were in alignment with the Race Guardian Angels and received guidance and also encouragement for their people. The Race Guardian Angels worked with the birth of life-waves in tribes and races, and with the withdrawal of such life-waves. They made it possible for men to make the transition from tribal characteristics to distinctive racial characteristics.

TRIBAL-ATOMS

In tribal-genesis each tribe is encased in an etheric encasement or a communal effluvia commanded by a tribal-atom. The tribal-atom determines the specific aim of the tribe. Under the compelling influence of its particularizing tribal-atom, the tribe ceases its nomadic wanderings, builds villages and sets up communal laws. Wherever there is communal life with one chief, and wherever men worship tribal gods, such men are encased in a tribal-atom. There are many in the world today who are yet encased in tribal-atoms.

The tribal-atom determines how men in the tribe affect one another. In certain tribes men express protective instincts for their young.

When the tribal-atom ceases to sound its central tone, the etheric encasement begins to disintegrate; tribal men abuse their wives and neglect their young; they refuse to hunt, and they practice cannibalism. The sexual taboos are ignored, and promiscuity is practiced in the tribe. Eventually, the tribal-atom ceases to sound its tone—and the etheric encasement disintegrates.

Tribal men who despoil the tribal honor and offend their taboos move in slower rhythms of reincarnation. When they return to the physical world, they are obnoxious agitators wherever they find themselves in the world. They refuse to respond to the upward rise of creation. They have a deep sense of self-guilt and therefore feel themselves to be inferior to other men. They expect other men to be responsible for them. They come into the world impudent and imprudent. They think the world owes them a living. They are laggards and parasites. Fortunately for such laggard ones, there are merciful helps in the world. Men having mercy and love sense the cause of their suffering. Their hidden hates and hostilities are forgiven by those who aid them through a blind mercy or charity. Though blind-mercy aid is not always helpful to one having an obstinate will, there are some who respond, and through this the gradual rise in genesis is made possible.

Rise in genesis demands that one be more

responsible, and that he use higher frequencies in thought, in emotion, in action. From responsible works, individualistic man is perfected.

God willed it that all men rise. Men who refuse to move with the crest of evolvement in genesis or in person bring sorrow to their environments and delay the fulfillment of their souls' purpose on earth. In the Bible these resisting men are spoken of as Cain, as Saul the king, as Judas, as Ananias, as Herod, as Pilate. This danger may be seen in all agnostic men of the present time. An atheistic heart becomes the victim of the heavy downpulling currents in the octave of pain centered in the earth. A hardened heart invites humiliation. An unresponding will attracts enslavement. An unteachable and disobedient mind comes under the influence of men who give untruthful and unethical instruction.

To unravel the flaming thread of life and weave it into comprehension is to understand the various stages of evolvement, and of the seemingly unending processes making up the personality and individuality of man.

One who would aid, heal, and instruct should look with reverence and wisdom into the liferecord of this eternity. Through grace he will be given the history of man's ancient origin and of the life-thread of survival through countless lives and expressions, beginning at the tribal and slowly evolving through the ages to produce the present personality.

> And when he (the priest) hath made her to drink the water, then it shall come to pass, that, if she be defiled, and have done trespass against her husband, that the water that causeth the curse shall enter into her, and become bitter and her belly shall swell, and her thigh shall rot: and the woman shall be a curse among her people. And if the woman be not defiled, but be clean; then she shall be free, and shall conceive seed.
> —Numbers 5:27,28

The Biblical passages in Numbers, Chapter 5, verses 12-31, portray the work of the priest in tribal-genesis with the Angels of Judgment and the Tribal Propagation Angels. Each sacred taboo protecting the tribe and race contained a degree of cursing. The Angels of Judgment and the Tribal Propagation Angels gave the priest in tribal-genesis the power of direct cursing. Members of the tribe who had committed adultery could be made sterile by the cursing of the priest, so that they would not pollute the tribe with contaminated offspring. Protective laws through the Judgment Angels exist in some degree in every genesis. Where there is profane or lustful action in sex, this is suffered "unto the third and to the fourth generation." (Exodus 34:7).

As men evolved through the ages into higher geneses, the power of cursing changed from the priest to the conscience of the individual. When this occurred, promiscuous and irreverent acts began to manifest sicknesses and painful ailments in the area from the thighs to the hips or the region of the loins.

Pain and suffering are more quickly invoked in offences against the generation or procreation act than in any other act in the lives of human beings. The higher the genesis evolvement, the greater is the penalty for an amoral life. Chronic ailments, weaknesses and conditions centered in the thighs, the generative organs, the rectum, or the lower intestines are the result of some unbalanced generative actions of this life and former lives.

> And Jacob was left alone; and there wrestled a man with him until the breaking of the day. And when he saw that he prevailed not against him, he touched the hollow of his thigh; and the hollow of Jacob's thigh was out of joint, as he wrestled with him.
>
> —Genesis 32:24,25

The "man" in this Biblical passage was the tribal-genesis *dweller,* who touched the hollow of Jacob's thigh because the thighs are the initiatory center of the genes in tribal-genesis and lesser family-genesis. In Jacob's wrestling with the dweller, the initiatory center of the thighs was shifted to the heart, so that Jacob, in future lives, might be reborn to a higher genesis. All persons undergo initiations through the area of the loins previous to expressing the next stage of genesis.

> **And he said, thy name shall be called no more Jacob, but Israel: for as a prince hast thou power with God and with men, and hast prevailed.**
>
> **—Genesis 32:28**

Jacob, through this dweller initiation and victory, received his sacred genesis-name of "Israel." In each transition between geneses, a person is given a new, sacred genesis-name by his Guardian Angel. Having concluded his former genesis, Jacob experienced a birth to the next genesis, and thus was given new vowels and consonants in his name, that he might more freely express the coming genesis. Some examples in the Scriptures of name changes, preceding a rise in genesis, are as follows: Abram to Abraham, Simon to Peter, Saul to Paul.

Jacob was called "prince"—meaning an adept of the etheric laws. The man "blessed him" (Genesis 32:29), signifying that Jacob's experience with the tribal-genesis dweller was consummated victoriously. Following this initiation Jacob met Esau, and their meeting was loving and harmonious, revealing that the tribal debts between him and his brother were resolved. (Genesis, Chapter 33)

Before Jacob had his encounter with the tribal-genesis dweller, he had begun his release from old tribal claims by detaching himself from the tribal possessivism of Laban, his father-in-law. Jacob received guidance, in a dream, to leave Laban, his father-in-law. (Genesis 31:11-13) Laban also had a dream which withheld him from restraining Jacob. (Genesis 31:24)

David offended both the purification laws of generation and the Life Fiat, in that he coveted the wife of Uriah and was responsible for the death of Uriah, so that he might take Bathsheba as his wife. The result of his actions was the death of the first child from their union, as the law of an eye for an eye or retribution, working with the Angels of Judgment, condemned David for his lustful acts. In the loss of his child, David suffered for his deviation. When men pervert the generative laws with their lusts and their self-wills, the result is tragedy and death.

Solomon had the power of manifestation; therefore, he had the power to magnify and multiply his possessions on an extravagant scale. His acquiring of vast territories and great quantities of silver and gold denotes manifestation knowledge. Yet due to the practice of polygamy, he retained something of tribal-genesis within himself. Therefore, he shut himself away from greater initiatory powers. Solomon's life is the example of "so far and no farther"—for some persons in the world may attain much wisdom, but they act emotionally through their tribal-genesis feelings. Such persons are unable to have access to the celestial archetypes, or the power "to go in and out."

In the extended cycles of re-embodiment or reincarnation, one gradually moves from one genesis level to another.

In the early stages of tribal-genesis, traits such as hatred, fear, and rivalry were necessary protective measures to produce certain strength capacities needed to master the forces of Nature and the animal world. However, when these traits, natural to tribal-genesis, are retained by men who are beginning to develop the cunning will and cunning mind in human- or family-genesis, rather than being natural traits, they become fierce traits dangerous to mankind.

Tribal-genesis and lesser human-genesis had both reached a decadent stage when Jesus came into the world. It is when these decaying periods are experienced in the earth that great Saviour action is made possible. In such a time came Jesus, as Saviour and Messiah, to give men "the way, the truth, and the life."

All men in human-genesis and in the earlier stages of self-genesis are colored by primitive traits. Some of these traits create a very real combat area in evolvement. Others move in subtle or insinuative manners; and others are shadow-like. But all or each of these may stand between a person and his higher evolvement. One should never underestimate the danger of these hidden primitive compulsions within. It is the work of the spiritual seeker to resolve the atavistic root-traits which would possess him during certain intervals or crisis periods of his life. Until he has resolved these ancient etheric compulsions within, he will be their servant rather than their master. If one indulges in even a remnant of hatred, this remnant will stand between him and the Light. The work of each person in the earlier stages of self-genesis is to face fearlessly any lingering or remaining negation root-traits of tribal-genesis and human-genesis within himself, and to recognize them for what they are. Before one may evolve to higher labors of the soul, he must determine the "what I am," so that he may become the "I Am."

THE PROTECTION OF THE ANGELS

In the latter part of every ten thousand years, the angelic protective veils encasing tribes, races, and nations are lifted so that men on all levels of evolvement may become penetrable to one another. In the present age, men are being given the opportunity to sustain this note of penetrableness. Should they fail, the angelic veils will descend and once again isolate tribes, races, and nations to their own means of evolvement. When these veils or etheric encasements encompass and seal in the tribes, races, and nations of the world, there are great divisions and separations.

Men encased in tribal-atoms cannot make alignment with their personal angels; and they do not express through family-atoms. But when men in races are established in their work through nations rather than through tribes, they then express themselves within family-atoms.

The Race Guardian Angels give the commandments and laws for preserving the morals of the race. These moral protections replace the sacred taboos formerly observed in tribes. During the time of Moses, the Race Guardian Angels, working with Jehovah, the Race-Lord, gave Moses the Ten Commandments.

The Recording Angels, working with the archetype of nations, are the spiritual chronologists of nations. They record the purpose and intent of a nation, and record the valorous and heroic events in a nation. They retain the historical records of nations so that patriotism may be sustained.

The Judgment Angels work with the destroying principle and the power of de-manifestation as a checkrein over the ambitions of tribes, races, and nations. The Judgment Angels arouse the dweller-entities representing the composite evil of tribes, races, nations, and lesser human-genesis families.

Every ten thousand years laggard souls have an upsurge of reincarnation. The etheric encasements which restrain them in races, in nations, and in family-atoms are lifted or loosened, that these souls may be free to move into other streams of reincarnation or re-embodiment.

Many persons who are laggard and who have been retained in semi-twilight states in the interior worlds are released to birth in this period of etheric-encasement lifting. Vast numbers of souls are released into the world, producing a population explosion. This is occurring in the present time, as men are ending a ten-thousand-year period.

In the stimulus of increasing evolvement, laggard souls produce agitation and great pressures, forcing men to enlarge their capacities. When this occurs, men are confused—and they understand not what is occurring in the world. They do not know that this is God's way of sweeping wayward souls into the earth, that these souls may have once again the opportunity to express themselves. Thus, they move in masses and numbers, and the population abounds throughout the earth. When a population explosion has fulfilled itself, all souls who have attained a higher degree of evolvement will express themselves in coming lives in a higher degree of the human spirit. Those who prefer to be agitators and dissenters are withdrawn after death into twilight states, where they will remain until another ten-thousand-year reincarnation tidal wave will sweep them into the world.

Wherever polygamy is practiced, it signifies that tribal-genesis is active. When men choose many wives, this is tribal-genesis action. In the Old Testament, tribal-genesis may be defined and recognized through the practice of taking several wives. Polygamy occurs only through tribal-genesis compulsions. The Tribal Procreation Angels direct these mating compulsions. When the Tribal Procreation or Propagation Angels withdraw their action, polygamy is no longer practiced. In the present time, wherever polygamy is practiced, it is tribal-genesis action.

INTERRACIAL MARRIAGE

Interracial marriage is a karmic situation in the present age, inflicting karmic heaviness upon those who choose to enter into such marriages. Interracial marriage produces a tremendous pressure upon those who marry. These marriages cause the conscience memory of the family-atoms within the race to be more intense. And more sacrifice is demanded in the personal lives of the husband and wife who consummate an interracial marriage.

As men reach the higher degrees of self-genesis there will be less thought of interracial marriage. Races are not dispersed through interracial marriage, nor will the racial problems be solved or resolved through interracial marriage.

When an individual chooses a mate of a different race, the karma in the marriage rests solely upon the individuals in the marriage. No one has the right to judge or condemn an interracial marriage. Such marriages occur because of the need to balance the debts of one's soul.

There is a greater law, however, determining racial experience. God's Equation directs racial appointment. When a person dies and prepares to be reborn, he re-embodies or reincarnates into a race or a nation where the particular theme of his soul will direct him and where he will best express his gifts and qualities. This is the way God maintains the greater equilibrium among races.

God placed Angels of Judgment and Angels of Propagation over all races. These protective Angels are still active in the world. They determine the timing when men or women resolve their generation debts through interracial marriage.

When the etheric encasements are lifted, it is more likely that interracial marriage will occur between those of widely divergent races. When men marry into races having extremely divergent cultures, this is the beginning of the decay of racial purity. Races which are more dissimilar in their cultures or in their soul evolvement produce greater restrictions as to karma and as to dweller action within the family or tribe.

Where racial barriers are extremely wide, there is more karma for the children produced from such marriages. Persons who intermarry in races which are closer in soul-tone or closer in atom evolvement are more likely to marry with happiness and with harmony. Such persons sometimes give birth to great egos, or children having something of a genius strain gathered from both lines or racial streams.

GENESES TRAITS

Tribal-Genesis	Lesser degrees Human-Genesis	Higher degrees Human-Genesis	Lesser degrees Self-Genesis	Higher degrees Self-Genesis
Courage	Bravery	Fearlessness	Daring	Renunciation. *"Whosoever will lose his life for my sake shall find it."* St. Matthew 16:25
Crude	Reformed	Refined	Sensitive	Soul Health. *"Be ye therefore perfect, even as your Father which is in heaven is perfect."* St. Matthew 5:48
Cupidity	Avariciousness	Acquisitiveness	Contemptuousness	Stewardship. Repect of others' belongings. *"For what is a man profited, if he shall gain the whole world, and lose his own soul?"* St. Matthew 16:26
Curse	Oath	Vow	Promise	Covenant. *"If any man will come after me, let him deny himself, and take up his cross, and follow me."* St. Matthew 16:24
Fear	Cunning-Will	Cunning-Mind	Manipulation	Death to the Primitive Will. *"Father ... not as I will, but as thou wilt."* St. Matthew 26:39
Fervor	Zeal	Ambition	Initiative	World-serving. Humanitarian.
Fortitude	Endurance	Stamina	Mastery	Overcoming. *"Be of good cheer; I have overcome the world."* St. John 16:33
Greed	Jealousy	Covetousness	Speculation	Acceptance. *"For he that hath, to him shall be given."* Mark 4:25

Tribal-Genesis	Lesser degrees Human-Genesis	Higher degrees Human-Genesis	Lesser degrees Self-Genesis	Higher degrees Self-Genesis
Hatred	Animosity	Prejudice	Critical-Mind	Consideration. *"Therefore all things whatsoever ye would that men should do to you, do ye even so to them."* St. Matthew 7:12
Honor	Character	Integrity	Standard	Ethic. *"Inasmuch as ye have done it unto one of the least of these my brethren, ye have done it unto me."* St. Matthew 25:40
Indigent	Dependent	Competence	Independence	Worthiness. *"By their fruits ye shall know them."* St. Matthew 7:20
Instinct	Apprehension	Foresight	Intuition	Seeing clear and true. *"If therefore thine eye be single, thy whole body shall be full of light."* St. Matthew 6:22
Isolation	Hypocrisy	Bigotry	Unteachableness	Illumination. The perceiving heart and the discerning mind.
Labor	Duty	Responsibility	Self-sustaining	Grace works. *"Labour not for the meat which perisheth, but for that meat which endureth unto everlasting life."* St. John 6:27
Lethargy	Slothfulness	Inhibited	Indifference	Gratitude. Impartial appreciativeness.
Lust	Lasciviousness	Sensuousness	Lack of self-control	Purity. *"Blessed are the pure in heart."* St. Matthew 5:8
Malice	Persecution	Gossip	Slander	Logos. Chaste speaking.

Tribal-Genesis	Lesser degrees Human-Genesis	Higher degrees Human-Genesis	Lesser degrees Self-Genesis	Higher degrees Self-Genesis
Pride of tribe or race	Pride of blood or stock	Pride of possessions	Pride of intellect	Humility. "The Father that dwelleth in me, he doeth the works. St. John 14:10
Primitive, possessive love. (children and wives are as chattel)	Personal, possessive, jealous love. (husband or wife feels "ownership" of mate)	Love of possessions	Self-love	Selflessness. "A new commandment I give unto you, That ye love one another." St. John 13:34
Rage	Anger	Antagonism	Indignation	Self-control. "Bless them that curse you." St. Matthew 5:44
Revenge	Vindictive	Retaliation	Self-righteous actions	Forgiveness. "If ye forgive not men their trespasses, neither will your Father forgive your trespasses." St. Matthew 6:15
Rivalry	Opponents	Competition	Strategy	Victory through initiation. "Agree with thine adversary quickly." St. Matthew 5:25
Treacherous	Timidity	Self-doubt	Egotism	Self-denial. Willing sacrifice for others.
Tribe or race as self	Family as self	Personality as self	Self-importance	Soul-equanimity. Selflessness.
Trust	Blind-faith	Belief	Proof	Prescience. Niscience or knowing.
Vulgarity	Irreverence	Reverence	Imbalanced judgments	Pure perception. "Judge not, that ye be not judged." St. Matthew 7:1
Will to survive	Will to live	Will to experience	Will to express	Serving as a Mediator. Will to serve.

6

PROTOTYPES

When continents shall be vicinities of proximity, the Eternal One and the human spirit shall blend as one. When the stars have ceased to be clusters to man, but each star has a pattern as the lines on the hand, then shall men observe the rules and the laws of God's Cosmos Plan. Once again men shall lean upon the angelic helps. And the human spirit shall bring the mysteries into the miraculous, and the miraculous into the visual. The human spirit shall produce the perfect prototypal man, a creator and craftsman for God. The human spirit shall produce a universal oneness, a peace-tongue which speaks in pure logos. Ancestral patterns shall be sealed away from men. The Lord Jesus shall be in His reign; and men shall be "like Him" and see Him once again.

SYMBOLS

There is a language of Heaven; the soul knows this language. It is a language communicable to the soul of man as a person, to the soul of man as a race, and to the soul of man as a nation. When men are equal in the light, they understand this language; their greatest deeds and their noblest acts come forth—and they stand at the pinnacle of God's Plan for them.

The language understood by the chiefs, priests, and matriarchs in tribal-genesis was a language of symbols. They understood their symbols through psychic, atavistic pictures, and etheric forms. The tribal Guardian Angels communicated their protective symbols to the women in the tribe who were preparing to bear children.

Signs, omens, and taboos were the outer language expressed or extended through symbols. The culture in tribes was transmitted through etheric symbology and through higher corrective symbology directed by the Recording Angels of the tribe. The Judgment Angels over the tribe also had their theme of symbology; through these symbols the laws of retribution were maintained.

The priests transmitted religious symbols to their tribal members through the use of certain images drawn on clay or through markings left on mountains or rocks. They also observed certain symbolic rituals portrayed through fire or through the sound of drums. Tribal speech contained many variations of these symbols and sounds.

Men who understood the etheric tribal symbols used stones and metals for certain protective amulets; they also used atavistic-symbol ritual to sustain the primitive etheric fire concealed within the amulets of protection. The talisman amulets of ancient times were known by the priests and chiefs of the tribes to hold potent magical power. The belief in amulets stems from tribal memories of primitive symbolic initiations passed down from one generation to another.

It was known by the priest, the medicine man, and the members of the tribe that if a man mastered a particular thing, he received a talisman symbol. If he mastered feats of strength, he would receive his symbol. If he mastered feats of daring, or brought courage and protection to the tribe, this produced a communal symbol which was added to the vocabulary of the tribe. Thus, the origin of communication came through symbology, which was in turn decoded by the priests and chiefs of the tribe.

In lesser family-genesis, priests and prophets in religious cults, working with higher levels of symbology, established the religious symbols and rituals known even in the present time. Thus, they kept alive the religious worship resurgence within their flocks or congregations.

Family-genesis and lesser self-genesis symbols are sometimes colored by the atavistic and animistic symbols carried over from the tribal-genesis memory of symbology, and by the religious symbols associated with the birth of individual conscience.

The most powerful symbols are the sacred symbols given to man through his own soul. The sacred symbols are received by man to mirror his relationship to God, to his conscience, and to his actions or works. Many of these symbols appear in dreams. Dreams are a part of the soul's revelatory stream. Men remember tribal symbology in dreams; they also experience family-genesis symbology in dreams. The majority of dreams are forms of self-evaluation, correction, and instruction.

The personal angels of man use an angelic dream symbology to teach man, and to provide him with a form of apprehension and protection.

When one begins to move from lesser family-genesis to higher family-genesis, and to become more individually assertive, dream symbologies begin to fade from his mind. Unfortunately, he thinks that the belief in dreams is superstition; he depends more upon the literal action of his mind and upon what he experiences physically through his senses or materiality.

When one is approaching lesser self-genesis, he depends upon the range of human experience to teach him. In lesser self-genesis, one who is agnostic disassociates himself from dream instruction and interpretation. He loses communication with etheric symbology which has made it possible for him, instinctively, to know himself, as well as those associated with him. His beliefs, energies and resources are directed toward prestige goals and material success.

As one evolves into self-genesis, the symbology which has been so important to him in tribal and lesser family-genesis begins to re-enter his emotions and thoughts. The etheric symbologies dormant in the lower part of *Quelle* or *Center Q* at the base of the skull are activated. At the present time, these atavistic symbols are intensely interesting to psychiatry. These symbols, when analyzed, often show primitive repressions and traits. To a psychiatrist with a discerning mind, these symbols also prove that man has a conscience.

In higher self-genesis, one comes into communion with the spiritual aspects of his dream symbologies, and he becomes familiar with the trustworthy symbology of mediative action through dreams as well as through daytime action. He begins to communicate with the *etheric braille* of the Spiritual Worlds. From this he extends his knowledge of the world of the soul; he learns of the action of his soul, of the meaning of his soul, and particularly of the meaning of God. God's life in him is symbolized through the inspiration he gives to men in the world.

When men are united with their consciences
and with the symbologies of Heaven, they come
into spiritual health. As men evolve in the earth,
they will come to understand sickness, ailments,
discomforts, unhappiness; and they will also
come to understand the deviations from health
in the men around them. They will know a
world of the soul which has been closed to them
during the long, weary period of wandering
from tribal-genesis to family-genesis—and, finally, to self-genesis.

HIERARCHY

To relate oneself impersonally to all levels
of the human spirit—so that he may minister
to his fellow man without prejudice or bigotry—
one should look beneath the surface of that
which is seen outwardly as personality and
should seek to discern God's intent for man.

To have a better understanding of the basic
laws governing the earth, it is important to
understand the working of the world-soul atom.
The world-soul atom has an etheric field which
completely encompasses the earth, the sun, and
the planetary system. The world-soul atom is
kept alive by the great constellation rays and
energies working in conjunction with the earth,
thus making it possible for the Father and Hierarchy to direct their cosmos creation powers
through the sun, moon, and planets onto the

earth—and therefore, onto man. The world-soul
atom, working with the cosmos atom in the sun,
keeps the earth in its elliptical orbit. The world-
soul atom forms a geometrical field. This field
is referred to in the Bible as "the bosom of the
Father." (St. John 1:18) The rays and tones of
Hierarchy, working through the world-soul
atom, make it possible for men to have an infinite range of creation through differentiation
and diversity.

Jehovah's action is centered within the moon's
reflected sphere situated on the outer rim of the
electromagnetic belt around the earth. Jehovah
works with the world-soul atom to make it
possible for men to have tribes, races, families,
and nations. The planets, working with Hierarchy and the Ancient of Days through the
world-soul atom, make it possible for men to
develop the greater potentials in temperament.

The rays of the moon are commanded by the
Race-Lord Jehovah, who holds the clue to race
compulsions working through men in tribal-
genesis and lesser family-genesis. As long as
races are in the earth, some men will continue
to reincarnate in tribal-genesis and family-genesis through life-wave compulsions, or reincarnation tidal waves.

One of the faulty concepts in the minds of
some persons is that they are in a state of perfection. When one understands Hierarchy Me-

diation within the bosom of the Father, or world-soul atom, he realizes that each man of the earth is in a state of unceasing evolvement. To understand Hierarchy and the great power of Mediation is to broaden discernment, and to channel with receptivity that which Hierarchy speaks to the world.

Were it not for Hierarchy or the great Host, the Father, and the Archangels, man would be sealed away and isolated from the memory of the creation of this earth. These mighty Beings are the Mediators between the earth and all other eternity systems and galaxies. It is through Hierarchy's alignment with the eternals that man may link himself to the unceasing and infinite action of other eternities, worlds, galaxies—and to the myriad actions of greater cosmos.

In far ranges of space or distances beyond the earth and its planets are great starry bodies known in astronomy as zodiacal constellations. A Great Being or Hierarch is centered within each one of the twelve zodiacal constellations around the earth. In the beginning of the creation of the earth, these twelve Great Beings or Hierarchs—working with the Will of God, the Father, and the Christ—began their work of Mediation onto the earth. One may understand the mighty constellation presences of Hierarchy when he sees cosmos as one body in God and all eternity systems and constellations expressing the Spirit of God. When one confirms Eternal Mediation, he is qualified to become a mediator—human and spiritual.

At the present time, the range of man's intellect and perception is being extended into the cosmos as well as the cosmic. If one would relate himself to world serving, and if he sincerely desires to live a spiritual life, he will seek seriously to align himself with the eternals, that he may become a fortified server for a world-need—and also that he may not become stranded in the circumstances of tumultuous world changes and coming events.

Hierarchy, using their twelve prototypal tones, send etheric compulsions onto the earth through the world-soul atom in epochs, periods, and cycles. These compulsions compel man to reincarnate from life to life so that he may gather every degree of prototypal action in the earth as part of his experience in consciousness. These prototypal life-compulsions, which are given to man through the cyclic laws of reincarnation or repeated births, are received into the sacred atom of his heart.

Some men in the present age are seeking to enter into the Christ-impulse, and thus are becoming free from the world-soul atom compulsions. Since the coming of Jesus, the Christ Spirit has begun to absorb the world-soul atom.

Until men have aligned themselves with the Christ, they will continue to be subjected to the reincarnation compulsions working through tribal and racial life-waves. When men work directly with the Christ-impulse, they will cease to embody in life-waves and will begin to direct their own embodiment rhythms.

The Christ, until the coming of Jesus, worked with the Father, using the archetypal rhythms to send the greater ideas to earth. The Christ centered His Light into the Invisible Sun surrounding the physical sun. When Jesus transcended the race-karma of the world, the Christ Spirit pierced the core of the earth. The Christ now works to absorb the world-soul atom, so that all men may have the opportunity to receive His Light.

Our Father of this eternity works *with* the Christ. The Christ will take over the Father's work when the world-soul atom compulsions have been entirely absorbed by the Christ archetypal impulse. This is what Jesus meant when He said, "My Father worketh hitherto, and I work." (St. John 5:17) When this occurs, men will be as sons of God or will have a creative consciousness similar to that of Hierarchy. "Is it not written in your law, I said, Ye are gods?" (St. John 10:34)

Those who now enter the self-genesis phase of evolvement are beginning to aid the Christ in the assimilation and absorption of the world-soul atom. From this will come the heaviest labors in evolvement.

The world-soul atom compulsions, which stimulate and direct generation through tribes and personality through families, are now being changed due to the Light of the Christ. This brings a decaying action to the etheric encasements surrounding tribal-genesis and lesser family-genesis. Men will have a greater and more noble relating to one another once they have made alignment with the Christ-impulse.

The world-soul atom compulsions will continue in the earth through millions of persons bound to tribal and racial compulsions. When cosmos-genesis has been established, all souls will be weighed. Those who have refused to evolve will be sealed into a twilight state, where they will remain until the end of this eternity.

> When the Son of man shall come in his glory, and all the holy angels with him, then shall he sit upon the throne of his glory: And before him shall be gathered all nations; and he shall separate them one from another, as a shepherd divideth his sheep from the goats: And he shall set the sheep on his right hand, but the goats on the left. Then shall the King say unto them on his right hand, Come, ye blessed of my Father, inherit the kingdom prepared for you from the foundation of the world.
>
> —St. Matthew 25:31-34

The creation story of this eternity as related to the form of man, to his repetitive reincarnation cycles, and to his intent on earth, can only be discerned through understanding the work of Hierarchy, the Father, the Christ, and the great Angels accompanying their labors. Hierarchy has command of the reincarnation compulsions through twelve prototypal actions, for the twelve Hierarchs command the twelve prototypal blueprints for man. "Let us make man in our image, after our likeness." (Genesis 1:26) The Hierarchs now work with our Father and the Archangels to send to mankind the reincarnation life-wave compulsions. They also "time" these life-waves to the earth, correlating them to the archetypal impulses or intelligible ideas sent to the earth by the Son of God, the Christ.

THE PROTOTYPAL CLIMB

In the Old and New Testaments may be found references to the upward rise in the prototypal climb. The twelve sons of Jacob represent the tribal-genesis prototypes. The twelve prophets of the Old Testament of the Bible represent the family-genesis prototypes. The twelve disciples around Jesus represent the self-genesis prototypes. Each one of these twelve in tribal-genesis, family-genesis, and self-genesis is a prototypal reflection of Hierarchy. Men on earth today are seeking to blend and perfect these twelve prototypal resemblances and expressions within themselves, so that they may incorporate and blend all of these into one, and thus become the perfect and pure prototype, even as Jesus was perfect. When this has occurred, men shall be "like Him" (1 John 3:2)—for Jesus is the ultimate prototype which men may fulfill on earth.

Tribal-genesis men receive world-soul atom life-compulsions into their gonads and genes. Family-genesis men receive their life-compulsions from the world-soul atom into the sacred atoms of their hearts. The self-genesis man receives the world-soul atom impulses into the indestructible atom centered within his forehead. The higher self-genesis man will eventually unite his thoughts with the Christ Spirit, rather than with the world-soul atom—and he will become an apostle for God.

The world-soul atom works through direct compulsions in nomadic or tribal-genesis, and is less direct in family or human-genesis. It works indirectly in the earlier phases of self-genesis. In the beginning of self-genesis, men contest these compulsions so as to bring forth an individualistic mental action. In the first phases of self-genesis, men undergo initiatory ordeals through the pressures of the world-soul atom. These ordeals are experienced that one may die to the primitive and atavistic compulsions and be born to an individualistic mentality under the Christ.

THE INDIVIDUALISTIC ATOM

In human-genesis or family-genesis, man establishes religions, education, cities, governments, nations. He seeks God through personal relating and interpretations. He personalizes God and worships Him as a personal Deity. In some instances, he may become a religious leader, an educator, a statesman; his authority is directed toward the good of humankind. In human-genesis, his nation is contested by wars with other nations. Through wars, he dissolves former race and family soul-debts, and strives to balance the racial impulses in the world.

Men in human-genesis who cling to tribal impulses use the cunning mind and cunning will to instigate wars, thus endangering that which has been built in previous ages.

In the first part of human-genesis, one alternates his sex from male to female; however, he reincarnates from one life to another in a slightly quickened timing. In the latter part of human-genesis, a woman may remain in a feminine body, or a man may remain in a masculine body, for many successive lives—until a certain quality is perfected.

Soul-debts are balanced in a more sensitized manner in human-genesis. The law of attraction is accelerated, and man begins to meet his destiny on more individualistic levels. Without deviation, the pendulum of retribution attracts to each one the results of that which he has sown. Thus, the opportunity is given to each one to resolve his own soul-debts.

The purpose of family or human-genesis is that man produce a personality. The personality is not self-created; it is a product of the ages. The personality of each man is produced by the thread of both reverent and irreverent tribal and family associations through countless ages. Even though the personality changes from life to life, the various memories brought forth from previous lives determine the field of personality experience and physical conduct in each life. It is the memory of physical action that determines man's physical conduct in each life. It is the memory of his personality associations that determines how great or how small the field of his personality experience may be in each life. Until man acquires reverence, his personality will express aggressiveness and hostility.

Associations in family ties, competitive aggressiveness in the outer world, and wars between nations enable man to produce an individualistic atom in his emotional body. This atom enables him to express a certain degree of intelligence in which the emotions are predominant. In human-genesis, man's ideal is preservation of the family. Thus, he expresses his thinking, emotionally, through the emotions and feelings of the family. Family and blood relationships are repeatedly experienced until perfection is brought forth as to the ideal in human association. The individualistic atom in the emotional body enables man to stabilize his emotions and to express his personality through the family, so that he may become reverent. It is the purpose of the whole family association that he acquire reverence. When he has attained reverence, he becomes an outstanding personality and, therefore, more helpful to humanity at large.

The emotional body atoms of man are now the determining factor as to his evolvement. Some on earth have evolved only the five lesser or sentient atoms of the emotional body; others have evolved seven; and, in some rare instances, ten. During certain intervals, the individualistic atom becomes an agitator to the atoms within the physical, emotional, and mental bodies. Through this agitation, man is initiated into a greater degree of consciousness.

If a person has but five sentient atoms activated in his emotional body, the agitation caused by the individualistic atom will result in some form of violence to, or suffering in, the physical body; some form of emotional tension in the emotional body; and some form of disturbance in the thoughts. If a person has activated seven emotional body atoms, the individualistic atom's effect upon the physical, emotional, and mental bodies opens the door of initiation to the Spiritual Worlds and to the spiritual life. If a person has activated ten emotional body atoms, the individualistic atom produces a heavenly recognition of him as a personage or a holy presence in Heaven and on earth. The individualistic atom in the emotional body of a holy person enables him to re-embody on earth if he so desires, or if there is need for his presence on earth.

Until man has produced twelve atoms in each body, the individualistic atom will continue to agitate, stimulate, and stir the other atoms in the various bodies. The purpose of the individualistic atom is to make man aware of his soul and of Heaven. As long as the individualistic atom is active, there is heavenly hope that man will seek a way out of materialistic and sensual expression.

Jesus of Nazareth was free from personality and its expression because His perfection needed not experience in this earth. The personality is solely for man's experience through tribal or nomadic-genesis, family or human-genesis, and in the earlier stages of self-genesis. When man has fulfilled self-genesis, he shall have perfected individuality—that is, his particularizing course of action for this eternity. Personality and individuality shall cease to be the chief actors on the stage of the drama of life. Man will have absorbed tribal instincts, personality, and individuality into his higher self—and he shall become a Being on earth.

The individualistic atom is the clue to experience and consciousness. Were it not for man's individualistic atom in each of the first three geneses, all atoms within his bodies would remain latent, dormant, or laggard, and he would be devoid of any self-directed action. He would be wholly influenced by mass impulse, and thus the initial purpose of this eternity would be defeated; for it is necessary that man, in the first phases of his evolvement, become individualized, so that he may eventually fulfill a unique kind of hierarchy work on earth.

A person may be out of alignment with his individualistic atom either temporarily or for many lives. If so, he is caught in a vacuum-like state. For example, when one in nomadic-genesis is sealed away from the individualistic atom in his physical body, he becomes a weakling in the eyes of the tribe. In human-genesis, when one is out of alignment with the individualistic atom in his emotional body, he becomes an indecisive personality, unable to love in any degree. He is non-self-reliant, therefore parasitically inclined, and is dependent upon family and family opinion. When faced with vital issues, such persons fail; as their structure is no stronger than that to which they relate themselves in their family association. If one in self-genesis is out of alignment with the individualistic atom in his mental body, he is unable to organize his thought processes or to think with clarity or justice.

When a person is said to have a magnetic personality, he is expressing the individualistic atom of his emotional body. When a person is thought to be of a pure intellect, and his character is fortified by wisdom and truth, he is in alignment with the individualistic atom of his mental body.

7

FAMILY-ATOM

It is holy to commune with God's creation, to know His way and Will for man. To know His love for each living thing is to come close to the center of His heart. To know His universe is to know Him. God has mapped or written His universe upon the souls of all knowing beings. When knowing has reached universal spiritual proportions, all is well with the heart, with the mind. The emanation of joy becomes as a radiant sun shedding its light upon everyone and everything. One may be happy while unknowing, but only with knowing may one know the holy joy.

Man is no stronger than that which he knows. When he knows God governs the universe through Laws and through His Will; when he is reverent, obedient, tender, ethical—he moves with the upward rise of his soul. He knows spiritual mediation Is. He knows God Is. And he lives in the physical world to assist others to rise. He assists others through various methods of instruction, charities, helps, understanding, forgivingness, and love.

The spiritual person comes to understand eternal patience. He sees that all men at one time or another are slow to respond to the rhythm of their souls. He sees that men have lived in this eternity for millions of years and, through progressive stages of evolvement, they have been hewn out, carved out, as fine stones or sculpture. Tribes, families, persons, society, religion, all forms of culture have shaped them. Disasters, crises, calamities have challenged them.

In nomadic or tribal-genesis, man is but one cell in a tribal nucleus. He struggles through the ages to produce an instinctual will through the use of the senses; he is supported by the primordial, etheric elemental forces, the tribal conscience, and the omniscient Beings governing the world-soul atom. He worships the forces of Nature. After many lives he begins to bring forth the individualistic atom of his physical body, thus either becoming a tribal leader or benefiting from those who lead him. He remains in tribal-genesis until he has absorbed certain lessons of mercy, so that the urge for physical power, gained in his previous rise and achievement, may be tempered and balanced.

When the soul begins to withdraw from tribal action, one exerts the effort to free himself from the former tribal-genesis expression, and from the compelling influence of the world-soul atom.

He establishes communities, villages, and becomes encased in a family-atom; his relationship to his offspring begins to be more refined. Through repeated trials in family association, he begins to produce personality as a vehicle for experience.

Until the coming of the Patriarchs, Abraham, Isaac and Jacob, men were solely dependent upon the world-soul atom and the tribal-atoms; all humanity on earth expressed tribal or nomadic-genesis. After the life of Jacob, men started their spiraling toward human-genesis or family-genesis; and those who were released from the tribal-atoms began their expression through family-atoms.

The complete life of Jacob is an initiatory story in which Jacob portrays the transition from tribal-genesis into human-genesis. (Genesis, Chapters 25 through 50) The story of Jacob reveals, in Jacob's marriage to Leah, a tribal-genesis action; and, in his marriage to Rachel, a human-genesis action.

The highest human-genesis action in marriage or mating is through pure love-choice, as in the case of Jacob and Rachel. "And Jacob served seven years for Rachel; and they seemed unto him but a few days, for the love he had to her." (Genesis 29:20)

A tribal-genesis relating in marriage exists when a mate is selected by family arrangement and custom, or by a karmic selection through the attraction of the senses. Jacob's marriage to Leah, arranged through the guile of Laban, her father, fulfilled a tribal custom.

> **And it came to pass, that in the morning, behold, it was Leah: and he said to Laban, What is this thou hast done unto me? did not I serve with thee for Rachel? wherefore then has thou beguiled me? And Laban said, it must not be so done in our country, to give the younger before the firstborn.**
> **—Genesis 29:25,26**

In the birth of Reuben and other children, through Leah and the handmaidens, Jacob became freed of certain tribal propagation compulsions. Leah, being in the tribal-genesis degree of evolvement, was the fitting recipient of the first seed of Jacob, as the first seed conceived in procreation action in all men carries the strongest tribal-genesis compulsion. It has been the custom in all ages to consider the firstborn the true heir; for the genes of the firstborn, containing a stronger ancestral survival instinct, hold the key to that which compels propagation, thereby assuring the perpetuation of the tribe or family.

When Jacob conceived Joseph through Rachel, he had reached a state in which his seed had become less tribal and atavistic; therefore, it was possible for the human-genesis gene to be manifested through the birth of Joseph. Joseph was not included in the twelve tribes of Jacob

because he was of human-genesis. In every family-atom there is one person more highly evolved
who is reaching toward a higher genesis—and
Joseph is an example of this. Benjamin, who
followed Joseph in birth, is the example of a
member of a family who has some of the characteristics of both human-genesis and tribal-
genesis. It was Benjamin's destiny, however, to
remain in tribal-genesis and to establish the tribe
of Benjamin.

There may be more than one degree of genesis
in each family-atom; and there may be one or
more persons in each family-atom who express
more than one genesis.

The child is always what the parents are in
the moment of conception, as this moment is
the time in which the purity or non-purity in
the procreative act determines what sort of person may enter the world. Lust or hate or fear
in the act of procreation will attract a fearful,
insecure person into the family environment.
Pure love and reverence in the time of procreation will attract a person joyful and loving, willing to serve in the world.

The pure love-impulse between two persons
in the act of procreation is used by the Higher
Worlds to bring forth a great personage to the
physical world. In the case of the Lord Jesus,
the seed which conceived Jesus was non-sensual,
uncolored by lust or passion.

It was the custom in the sacred and reverent marriage relatings between a highly evolved man and woman that they would fast, pray, and consecrate their act of procreation, so as to give birth to one of pure purpose for the world. In this way of serving it was felt that the one entering the earth might be a saviour of the world. Mary and Joseph were prepared in previous lives for their catalyst alignment with one another, and they were also prepared by the Essenes in the physical world to be the principals in the drama of parenthood for the Messiah or Lord Jesus.

There have been many questions pertaining to the other children conceived by Mary and Joseph. Historical records show that they were unlike their brother; the embodiment records confirm that they were unlike Jesus and portrayed the tribal-genesis and earlier human-genesis degrees of evolvement. It may be said that Joseph and Mary, after the birth of Jesus, produced a family similar to other families. Their children were congenial and also noncongenial. In all family-atoms there are egos expressing varying stages of genesis; this is necessary so that experience within a family-atom may be rounded out and proportioned.

Certain family-atoms attract souls having a very high degree of evolvement. However, these are rare instances and come from grace earned

in former lives of love and harmony. Highly
evolved persons are attracted to such *grace family-atoms* so as to bring pure individuals to the
world who will dedicate to aid mankind. Grace
family-atoms have both higher and lower aspects. Mary and Joseph, in bringing Jesus to
the world, used the higher aspect of a grace
family-atom.

When a spiritual person finds himself centered within a *fixed family-atom,* where karma
is intense, he finds that the first labors required
of him often demand that he work directly to aid
in the resolving of the family karma at hand.
His discipline is that he fulfill, without tension
or resentment, the responsibilities placed upon
him, and also maintain his individuality as to
his application toward a spiritual life.

The Lord Jesus came to show men how to
treat one another, how to look into the souls of
other men, how to cherish them as beloved
friends, how to answer their questions, and also
how to understand their follies.

Jesus was repelled by no human being. He
understood life generating in each man. He saw
the souls of men; He touched their souls—and
those who responded were quickened and transformed.

Jesus worked with tribes of men; He worked
with men who were rising into human-genesis
lives. He knew their hearts, but He knew there

was a greater man to come—a man who, as an individual, would become more and more a steward for God, and therefore a mediator with Heaven and a mediator for his fellow man.

ANGELS AND THE FAMILY-ATOM

The life within a tribal-atom is of a conglomerate nature, in that one tribal-atom affects a number of persons. The life within a family-atom is a concentrated action affecting a limited number of persons—and there is a magnified awareness of one another. Through joint association in karma, the individual traits of each person in the family-atom are singled out, yet the family as a whole seeks to accomplish for society a particular thing.

All men in lesser human-genesis are encased in family-atoms. When men emerge from the tribal-atoms into particularized family-atoms, they enter a more direct relating to the angelic world, as each family-atom is under the direct supervision of a Guardian Angel and a Recording Angel.

In the earlier stages of family-genesis, members of the family receive mercy helps from the Recording Angel and the Guardian-Angel of the family-atom. Men in lesser family-genesis are unable to make alignment with their personal angels, and must depend upon the guidance of the Guardian Angel of the family-atom.

The coming of Jesus made it possible for men
to receive a more sensitive ministering help from
the angels protecting the family atom; His coming also enabled men to penetrate and open the
grace aspect of the family-atom. "For the law
was given by Moses, but grace and truth came
by Jesus . . . " (St. John 1:17)

The Recording Angel of the family-atom records all of the good actions of the individuals
encased in a family-atom. The Recording Angel
enables the grace aspect to work as guidance for
the family. When the Recording Angel records
the good works of the family, the works of good
live to become potentials in grace.

As one evolves through the family-atom influence, he inherits the conscience of the family-
atom. Through this conscience aspect, which
works through the Recording Angel overdwelling the family-atom, he begins to incorporate
a compassion for the suffering of other men;
and, over the ages, a humanitarian attitude toward his fellow man begins to imprint itself
upon him. He starts a strenuous and deliberate
effort to purify the generation or procreative
stream. He begins to bring forth an individualistic atom within his emotional body. He revives
old etheric powers which he had in previous
lives. In some instances he may become prophet-
ically aligned with that which is beneficial for
his family or for the families in his environment.

He builds or contributes to a tabernacle, and observes sanitary laws and protective moral laws. He becomes obedient to certain religious rituals through which families worship.

When one makes alignment with the Guardian Angel and Recording Angel of the family-atom, he intuits the needs of his family—and he becomes directly responsible for the moral purity of his ties in blood.

The Father, who assigns a Guardian Angel and a Recording Angel over each family-atom, also provides each family-atom with a reflecting photographic etheric light. All wrongs committed by the family—selfishness, hostility, neglect, and moral abuse—are photographed upon this reflecting etheric light. This creates a family *dweller* action.

The sins of the fathers are recorded upon the etheric reflecting light in the family-atom. These sins are carried over "unto the third and to the fourth generation" (Exodus 34:7). Therefore, any child born with memory of sin or guilt on his soul will respond to the dweller compulsion in the family-atom—rather than to the angelic helps.

The moral and ethical standard of the family is sustained by the efforts of the family and through the combined work of the Recording Angel and the Guardian Angel of the family-atom.

The Guardian Angel of the family-atom works in a magnified mediative action. The prayers of a true mother for her family or for an individual in the family are supported by this mediative action; thus the prayers of a true mother are always answered in some degree. When there is a dweller experience in the family, the mother's prayers may modify the heavier impact of the karma.

The dweller of the family-atom reflects the negative actions of the members of the family who have been together in former lives, and also reflects the combined, negative actions of the family in this life. The dweller of the family-atom is the means through which a family is presented in ripe timing with certain griefs, sorrows, and disciplines, so that the family may be purged and cleansed. When the dweller's action is in alignment with the Guardian Angel and the Recording Angel of the family-atom, this becomes the voice of conscience in the family. (The dweller of the family-atom and the personal dweller of an individual are not the same.)

The family-atom conscience is reflected in the ancestral genes. This appears as reverence for the sexual act, or reverence for the holy vows of marriage. The family-atom conscience may also be expressed in the way the family uses its possessions or money, and how stewardship is preserved, or in the way a family looks upon the value of things. The family-atom conscience is also used by the Guardian Angel to show those in the family the meaning and cause in sickness, or the correcting discipline in the various lessons which are shared among the members of the family. The family-atom conscience reminds those in the family to be hospitable in their home, to invite the stranger in, and therefore to be prepared at any time to entertain an angel. The family-atom conscience especially reminds those in the family to keep alive the ties of blood through love, and to keep reverent and confident the stabilizing things related to family-life.

As men evolve in genesis, the family-atom sometimes seems to retreat; but as men evolve more and more in the spiritual side of their natures, the family-atom conscience speaks—so that they may revere the relationships in the family. Families who respond to the family-atom conscience retain in the higher side of their memories the good things of family life, that they may be preserved and written in the records of their individual souls, as well as in the records of the family-atoms.

When there is grace, the Guardian Angel of the family-atom protects the family from harm and danger. For instance, a member of the family may be warned in a dream as to some forthcoming danger to the family or one of its members.

There is invariably one person in the family-atom who is a grace-dreamer. This may be the mother, father, or one of the children. The grace-dreamer speaks for God's symbology, which would be placed before the sight of the family. Through grace-dreams the family receives a certain degree of apprehension and also correction which reinforces the moral laws supporting and sustaining the family. If a mother and father were more alerted to the spiritual significance or the higher symbology of the dreams of their child, they would better understand the child's hungers and desires; they would perceive the soul's revealing of the child's past lives. They would have the comfort, support, and guidance received from the conscience of the family-atom.

The family-atom conscience is very apparent in the dreams of the mother, father, or the children. The conscience of the family is a gathered grace from many, many lives of association in family life. The family-atom conscience contains the memory of the things one should do or should not do, or a warning tone from the combined tone of the souls in the family-atom. Through the family-atom conscience, families may prepare for certain hardships to come. The Guardian Angel and Recording Angel alert the conscience of the family, that the family may be prepared and fortified for things pleasant and unpleasant. It is family-atom conscience speaking through dreams when one is alerted, forewarned, or prepared for coming family events. All who have this grace in the family have earned the guidance of the family-atom Guardian Angel who guides them and protects them.

Through death of a father, mother, sister, or brother, members of a family-atom are weighed by the Guardian Angel of the family. Dissent over the way of burial and over the distribution of inheritance is registered upon the etheric sensitivity existing among members of a family-atom.

A family-atom has a *lesser etheric encasement* and a *higher etheric encasement*. The lesser etheric encasement is the karmic field of action and is overshadowed by the dweller of the family-atom. The higher etheric encasement is the grace aspect of the family-atom and is overdwelt by the Recording Angel and Guardian Angel.

There are five reasons why a family may be held or retained in the lesser etheric encasement of the family-atom: if there is some lingering of tribal-genesis; if the marriage is one of sensual attraction rather than pure love; if the marriage is of karmic attraction rather than grace attraction; if there still remains strong attachment to the wife's or husband's father or mother, and there is the failure to forsake all others; if there is heavy personal karma to be resolved between husband and wife.

If a husband and wife have a deep and reverent love, and have forsaken all others, they are encased in the higher etheric encasement of the family-atom.

As long as persons live negatively toward one another or express lust and base passions, they are isolated from the higher or grace aspect of the family-atom and are thrown entirely upon one another's resources, temperament, and character. In this, they fail to express the higher attributes of the family-atom.

When a man and woman enter into a pure state of love—and a true marriage is to be consummated—their alignment with the family-atom begins with the betrothal; the betrothed come in contact with the higher etheric encasement or grace aspect of a family-atom. Thus, they become the recipients of the help and the blessing of the Guardian Angel and Recording Angel, who directly overdwell the betrothal, the marriage ritual and ceremony, and the conception of children. The Recording Angel and the Guardian Angel of the family-atom work directly with the Propagation Angels. Therefore, the ideal function of marriage in family-genesis is the begetting of children.

When there is pure love between a man and woman, and a desire to be faithful to one another and loyal to the marriage vow, the marriage is a grace marriage. However, this marital grace must be sustained by continuing love actions, fidelity, and a nourishment of that which is expressed within the marriage.

Husband and wife who refrain from giving all of themselves to the marriage—being jealous, neglectful, distrustful, or over-possessive—attract heavy karma. A child conceived by such parents may be born in alignment with the dweller of the family-atom, and thus great lessons will be experienced through the addition of this child to the home. However, in all families there is the potential angelic blessing.

Prayer is the first means of penetrableness to the grace aspect of the family-atom. When prayer begins in a family, the family mitigates its karmic trials in the home. When prayers result in love and consideration for one another, the grace aspect of the family-atom is activated. However, there must be a continuing effort to maintain this grace alignment, as the many trials in the world are constantly challenging the close relationships of persons. Only through reverence, patience, deep knowing in faith, and spiritual understanding may the grace aspect of a family-atom be sustained.

If there is but one person in the family environment who prays to aid those in family-ties or association, the angels overdirecting the family-atom come forth in right timing and free the works of grace into the family action and expression. Regardless of how wayward, perverse or stubborn persons may be, there is someone in the family environment who can penetrate the higher aspect of grace, so that it may be channelled into the family at large. As a rule, this is the mother of the family; however, this person may be the father, or a child; or, it may be channelled through a condition in the family which necessitates prayer. Such prayers make penetration into the higher helps offered to each family in the world—for the Father so loves His children that He gives His angels to watch over them.

> Because thou hast made the Lord, which is my refuge, even the most High, thy habitation; There shall no evil befall thee, neither shall any plague come nigh thy dwelling. For he shall give his angels charge over thee, to keep thee in all thy ways. They shall bear thee up in their hands, lest thou dash thy foot against a stone.
>
> —Psalm 91:9-12

Each member of a family influences and affects, to some degree, all other members within the family-atom. When there are sicknesses, dissensions, trials; or when there is love, success, or brilliance expressed by any one member of the family, all are influenced in some manner. In event of an inverted action by one member of the family, all are affected negatively, and suffer.

Regardless of a karmic situation in a family, if there is prayer, within every sorrow there is a concealed blessing; within every weakness there is a hidden strength; and within every affliction and infirmity there is a potential healing.

The family-atom has three functions: the primitive filial, the human-genesis filial, and the individualistic. The *primitive filial* retains something of tribal-genesis. When the complete family functions in the primitive filial state, the result is a family introversion and retrogression, out of pace with society, inclined toward primitive ideas regarding possessions, morals, marriage, education, religion. The members of such families function through one another—feeling and thinking with blood-tie faculties rather than individuality. They look upon the outside world as the enemy.

The *human-genesis filial* is possessed by a common determination to compete with and exceed other families. These families seek to excel in the world for the good of the family name. They look upon the outside world as rivals.

The *individualistic* function of the family-atom is devoid of filial compulsion, and expresses a congenial or uncongenial separateness, as the case may be—thus affording each member of the family a freedom to pursue the talents lying close to the individuality. In such family-atoms, there may be those who are devoid of the feeling of responsibility as to the home and its survival, or there may be those who must bear alone the burdens of the less thoughtful members of the family. Those who are encased in the individualistic family-atom look for equality rather than competition.

The more highly evolved person is the product of a congenial or uncongenial separateness. He often finds himself with family ties and responsibilities expressing conflicting views as to morals, religion, and ethic.

When one dedicates himself to a spiritual life, his first initiatory trials pertain to the family-atom association. If he has in any manner failed to understand the family filial action, he must retrace his steps as to his attitudes toward those who have shared his intimate family environment, disciplines, and progressions. In these initiatory trials he learns to look beyond the family imagery; the ancestral perspective is shifted and changed. His spiritual insight will give him a wisdom beyond the accepted family pattern.

One who applies the "love ye one another"

ethic within the family sees the face of his brother, sister, father, mother, child, wife in a different light. The Guardian Angel of the family-atom will guide him to know the right timing of intimacy, and the suitable timing of privacy and releasing.

> Who is my mother? and who are my brethren? And he stretched forth his hand toward his disciples, and said, Behold my mother and my brethren! For whosoever shall do the will of my Father which is in heaven, the same is my brother, and sister, and mother.
>
> —St. Matthew 12:48-50

Each family in *higher family-genesis* works more directly with the angels of the family-atom. When there is an alignent with the Recording Angel and the Guardian Angel of the family-atom, the family may experience intervals of grace.

Men in higher family-genesis are in alignment with their personal angels and benefit from their helps, but they are not aware of these angels. The *personal Recording Angel* records one's pure actions, thoughts, and emotions from life to life, and preserves the medallion of grace around the soul. The *personal Guardian Angel* protects a person, and times one's greater initiations. The personal Guardian Angel also holds the key to the soul's pure record or medallion of grace, so that one may receive guidance through dreams and mediation.

The *Luminosity Angel* protects one's physical body and lesser etheric body; and also protects the sacred atom of the heart in waking, sleeping, birth, and death. The *Angel of Pure Desiring* works with the conscience aspect of the soul, and seeks to direct the love motive and intent of a person. The *Niscience Angel* works to keep the mental triad atoms of the mind in alignment with the Will of God, the Light of the Christ, and the Life of the Father. The Niscience Angel works that man, in the coming ages, may activate a fourth atom for the mental body. This fourth atom for the mental body will contain an omniscient cell, and thus will enable man to become co-atom to the Christ Mind.

PLANETARY TONE AND THE FAMILY

When the Father assigns certain souls to a family-atom, the axis-tones of a particular planet—on equal frequency with the soul-tones of those who are to dwell in the family-atom— take command of the family-atom. Thus, each family-atom receives its major planetary vitalities from one planet.

The planetary tones energizing a family-atom time the initiatory trials of the family, and thereby assist Hierarchy to shape and form the temperaments within a family-atom.

The more highly evolved members of a family-atom directed by the higher tones of Mars are brave, courageous, valiant, industrious, just, patriotic. In a family-atom influenced by the lower tones of the planet Mars, the family is militant and aggressive.

In a family-atom under the direction of Jupiter, the members of the family have a tendency to be enthusiastic, daring, generous, and original. In a Jupiter-tone family-atom, a child entering the world with heavy soul-debts is extravagant, parasitical, dishonest, and unscrupulous.

In a family-atom overdirected by the planet Saturn, the parents and the offspring live a restrained, disciplined, and often frugal life. Members of a Saturn family-atom become good historians, teachers, geographers, disciplinarians, traders, archaeologists, miners, mining engineers. The Saturn family-atom personality has an earthy wit and a homely sense of humor. The underlying theme is reverence for traditional and established procedure. The negative offspring influenced by the dweller of the Saturn family-atom may be mentally slow to learn, unappreciative of culture, plodding in his efforts, obstinate and impenetrable.

A Venus family-atom produces a versatile, artistic, harmonious, loving congeniality. Souls born to a Venus family-atom are as a rule beautiful in body and in features. Talents expressed are on the esthetic levels; expression is a reverence for beauty. The gross individuals in a

Venus family-atom are sensual, voluptuous, greedy, lustful, retaliative. They bring sorrow and shame to their family through the abuse of love and good taste.

In the Mercury family-atom are to be found more souls who are reaching for higher self-genesis. Such persons are inventive, creative, and articulate in the mental arts on all levels. Their pursuits are expressed in a vital quickness and response to all forms of association. The theme of a Mercury family-atom is reverence for intellect. The negative person of the Mercury family-atom expresses untruthfulness, slander, envy, spite, intrusion, irreverence, talkativeness; and he is inclined to use obscene and vulgar words.

Many family-atoms in the present time are under the influence of Uranus, Neptune, and Pluto. Persons in these family-atoms are ingenious, creative, independent, unpredictable. Their activities cannot be perceived or weighed by the ordinary analysis, as such egos are advanced souls who for many lives have expressed an accelerated mentality. From such souls will come the perfected self-genesis prototype.

8

MARRIAGE AND THE FAMILY

The magnetic forces of attracting and repelling are perpetually at work between man and woman. Selection of a mate is more than biological. One's choice of a mate is determined by the soul's need to expand its glorious potential into the human spirit. Regardless of one's concept of marriage, the great powers of the soul and the spirit work continually to make man's outer being equal to his inner being.

In the lesser self-genesis age, all partnerships in marriage or out of marriage are undergoing transition; for something is seeking to come to birth in a mighty polarity shifting. It is the divine intent that marriage shall come into a holy synthesis, and thereby establish a more ideal state of equal strengths and talents, thus producing a union of harmony and love.

In a synthesis-harmony in marriage, the bride and the bridegroom think upon one another as a fusing of the two into the one; they look to God to use their complementary attributes—loving emotional, creative mental.

The masculine and feminine polarities in all

persons are projections of spirit and soul. These seek to unite, that the higher progenies of creation or greater ideas may be born to the world.

When there is a perfect marriage on the physical plane, the angels can fulfill their work for the human family through those who truly love in the marriage state.

A person should not judge another person as to his selection of a mate in marriage. One who is spiritually evolved knows marriage to be a necessary state in the physical world—not only that men may produce children for the human spirit, but that man and woman shall be true helpmates united and made one against an alien world.

No one in the physical world ever escapes the law of diversity until he has attained the divine union in his inner nature between his soul and his spirit. Through the diversities one is shaped and formed; thus when one finds his similar in marriage, they share the diverse trials of the world. United against diversity, two persons living in the higher degrees of genesis become a solid front, exemplifying character, integrity.

All initiatory marriages are marriages of opposites in temperament. All synthesis-harmony marriages are marriages between those of similar nature.

Until men reach cosmos-genesis, the synthesis-harmony marriage will be a rarity. It is grace when one marries a similar, and thereby magnifies his own nature through the person he loves. When one is fortified by magnification of his own qualities through his mate, this is an anointed marriage.

When one looks into his interior nature, he begins to understand something of the dual and alternate polarities. Equalization of these dual powers within himself is prompted by the soul and the spirit. Until he has accomplished the equalization of the dual powers, marriage will remain an initiatory state. When one has finally interblended the powers of his soul and spirit with the powers of his emotions and thoughts, he will attract a mate of equal nature and equal temperament.

Every 7,000 years the polarity impulse changes in the marriage relationship. In the year of 1846 the masculine polarity emphasis governing marriage began to change to a feminine polarity emphasis. Women entered into more aggressive attitudes. Family-genesis relationships came under severe and disturbing internal stimuli.

In this age of science and the coinciding period of the lifting of the etheric veils between races, nations, continents, tribes, families, and individuals, there is something speaking from Heaven—and only Heaven can give the answer.

When the eternal nature of man is separated from his day-by-day action, this produces a situation abnormal in the natural rise of evolvement, and also produces extreme anguish for those who must suffer in their unknowing and their non-responding.

The pressures of the outer world should bring families closer together in these times. Unfortunately, in the scientific or lesser self-genesis age, the external urgencies seem to divide and make disunion in the family life. This is caused by the pressures placed upon the family-atom when persons would rise into higher geneses, and thus become more individualized.

Family-atoms are presently suffering internal and external pressures due to the extreme differences in prototypes and temperaments which are being incorporated into family-atoms through reincarnation. This produces an upset society, a decaying society, but in time will produce a more worthy society. It is natural and normal in God's Plan that these periods of stress and distraction occur simultaneously. They come that men may become more sensitive and alert, and also that men who so desire may have victory and gather greater resources in strength and intelligence—and thus produce a particular thing for God.

When God's creative fiat sounds upon a family-atom, this is the beginning of new habits and the discarding of old habits, attitudes, and conditions.

When families come to recognize progressive rhythms pressing upon them and also understand the cyclic orbits of change in family growth and evolvement, there will be much progress made in family life, and more understanding of one another.

The composite body of a family may stand for something in society, or it may be detrimental to society. If the father and mother are emotionally immature, their habits can disorient and imbalance their children's lives. Such families upset and disturb a community, and become poisonous elements in society.

The homes of people give a clue to the degree of soul evolvement within a family-atom. In each home there is an etheric atmosphere. A sensitive person visiting a home or household may immediately enter into the combined soul of the family emanating its thoughts and emotions, and take upon himself something of the restrictions or the freedoms within the family-atom. He may also intuit the karma within the family, the unhappiness and sorrow of the family which linger in the etheric atmosphere of the home. One may enter a house in which the family is absent and intuit where sorrow or tragedy has occurred. When one enters a home of purity—where joy and love have been expressed or fulfilled—this is a grace blessing, and can be healing to the visitor, wanderer, or stranger.

Husbands and wives have their own language—a language built out of their most intimate associations. If their intimate associations are sacred, there is an atmosphere of happiness and harmony in the home. If their intimacy has been abused or is imbalanced, the vitality in the home is a depleted or depressing vitality.

Husbands and wives who live for the rise in society alone, or who seek social goals for prestige, produce a charged, unrestful atmosphere in their homes. Highly evolved or sensitive children born to such families are emotionally starved; their vital emotional responses are curbed.

All emotional evolvement within the family-atom is dependent upon the love relationship between the husband and wife. If there is love for the offspring at the moment of birth, and if the parents comprehend what the child represents as a soul given unto them in stewardship—this is a blessing in the home; and the nurturing of love between the husband and wife is strengthened. If there is weakness on the part of a mother, in which she fails to assume the parental responsibility—neglecting the household or domestic tasks and failing in matriarchal authority—it is discouraging and devitalizing to the husband. This also brings about emotional con-

flict in the child, or a division in his emotional
response to his parents. Thereafter, as he
matures, his emotions and loyalties are inclined
to be biased and divided.

If a soul is born to a family where there is
much joy, this is grace. When a highly evolved
ego chooses to enter a family and bless it with
his genius, as well as with his pure reverence
of soul, this is sometimes unseen by a calloused
father or mother, and the child's genius is re-
pressed and ignored—or if the parents are unscrupulous, the child is exploited. Genius children often feel desolate in their childhood and
seek outside the family for other means of
security and support. In some instances this very
weakness on the part of parents inclines the child
to seek sources of spiritual nourishment.

When the etheric encasement surrounds a
tribe, the Agrarian Angels and the Propagation
Angels work with the mothers and the older
matriarchs of the tribe to enable children to receive their proper nourishment, to protect them
against the cold, and to give them resistance to
germs and disease. In the family-atom, if the
mother remembers the etheric laws, and responds to the help of the angels, she receives
intuitive helps in feeding her children and in
giving them nourishment suitable to the chemistry of their bodies. If a mother fails to unite
with the angels, her children become eccentric

in food habits and crave only devitalized foods.

If a mother who suffers from nervous tension is impatient or irritable at the table, an electrical atmosphere is immediately set up in the home; and the more sensitive children develop a neurotic attitude toward food, or look upon mealtime as a time of irritation. The memory of this irritation is sealed into their salivary glands and taste buds, and lasts into adulthood.

The stomach is the organ symbolizing the mother's love to her child. Even as an infant receives food from his mother's breast, the child intuits emotionally that he must receive food from her hands. The child looks to the mother as a restoring-life symbol in the home. In the inner mind of all adults, the mother is the symbol of restoring and giving life.

A mother who has the grace to be united with the angels overdirecting the chemistry of the bodies of her children is a mother blessed of God. If she intuits the need of the bodies of her children, she builds strong physical bodies, not only in her womb, but in the world. She also gives the child a chance to cope with the aggressions in the world. Children who are truly fed do not crave food, because they are fed and nourished by loving hands. Unappeased hunger in persons, producing obesity in later life, is caused by being undernourished by the mother-love, by irritations, scenes and quarrels at the table. Neurotic traits in appetite, or the desire to eat at unseemly hours—all stem from the fact of irregularity in the habits of the mother in giving food or substance to the child.

The father who brings the supply to the household, through which the mechanics of the home are oiled, establishes security in the minds of his children. Children who look to their father with assurance and pride are prepared to meet the world and its competitive challenges.

As men progress and evolve into higher stages of human-genesis and self-genesis, the father parent receives the full impact of the pressures in the materialistic and scientific world. Upon the father falls the burden of remaining to his children the ideal image representing "Our Father which art in Heaven." If the mother in any manner feels that the father has failed to meet the social standards as a provider for their children, she disassociates herself from the help of the angels over the family-atom; for the angels do not support the social ambitions of man, nor do they work to give social prestige to man. The angels support only that which is of the true and the real.

If the father fails to provide virile provisions for his family, and if he fails in his reverent attitude toward his wife, there is placed in the mind of the child a fear of the world itself—a fear of the intangible competitions existing in the outer world. The child, having before him the shattered ideal of his father, fears that he can never compete with this world. When this occurs, a family has intense need of spiritual nourishment. A family without spiritual nourishment is a family exposed to heavy dweller action.

If a family moves to another community or city, away from its familiar environment, the family is challenged as to its stability and the sincere communion among its members.

The lesser self-genesis person married to a person of family-genesis level of evolvement does not understand unison of ideas relating to marriage, children, and the home. Should the lesser self-genesis mate be the husband, the results would be an aversion to the purchase of a home or permanent residence, a neglect of marital demonstrativeness, and an indifference concerning the increase of children; in some cases, conceiving too many children without thought of the welfare or health of the mate. There is irresponsibility as to finances and the ordinary necessities of the family.

The lesser self-genesis husband, being more concerned with the drive of his ego, is not willing to sacrifice to protect his family, but accepts the sacrifice of his family and children as his just due.

When the mother is a family-genesis ego, and

is married to a lesser self-genesis ego, and if she desires the preservation of her children for the sake of her children and her home, she will undergo many painful marital initiations. Lesser self-genesis husbands, being unstable, often feel compelled to desert their wives and families— and thus be free of marital obligations.

Each marriage has its own individual equation which is subjected to unseen laws of correction and predestination. It is inevitable that a marriage fail if it is founded upon lust, faulty sentiments, immaturity.

A desire of one person to dominate the will of another in any relationship offends the law of God. In marriage, it is offensive in the eyes of God when one marital partner, knowing himself to be magnetically irresistible to his mate, uses this power to manipulate the soul of the one entrusted to him through marriage.

It is offensive to God and His law when a marriage partner is devoted to a father or mother parent rather than to wife or husband. It is also against the law of perfect partnership for a father or mother to show particular preference for one child in the family environment. The family-atom is offended when either parent would abnormally possess a child.

The sexual life is a natural life between man and woman when founded upon mutual love and trust of one another. It is offensive to God when husband or wife commits adultery in thought through flirtations, or through dwelling in sensuous thought upon a person outside of the marriage.

Miracles may be manifested in a marriage; such miracles usually begin with the woman. Until men reach higher self-genesis, the marital grace aspect is more often received through the wife. A woman who desires that her marriage be preserved, often preserves her marriage at the cost of sacrificing her own desires; sometimes she must close her eyes to the immorality or inferiority of her mate. In woman, the soul instills the preservation instinct; and, if she will, she can maintain the balance in marital harmony. This can be done through prayer— prayer accompanied by kindness, generosity, love, affection, humor, wisdom, reverence, and thoughtfulness.

If the husband holds the grace aspect of the marriage, a criticizing, carping wife is a drain upon his energy and vitality. She is a cancer to his ambition and progress. A man desires dignity and self-respect. If the most familiar person, his wife, finds fault with his good intent, he is humiliated; he is un-manned.

There is very often a competitive resistance between brothers and sisters. Many brothers and sisters are but casual associates or are indifferent to one another. They are indifferent because they have not known one another in former lives; they are newcomers to one another in a family-atom.

There are brothers and sisters who have a hypersensitive telepathic accord with one another; who think as one in the family-atom. Their combined association can be happy for the family, or at times it may bring unhappiness to the father and mother, or to other children in the family-atom. Such souls who have this combined telepathy in the family-atom have been sisters or brothers, and sometimes twins, in a former life; or they have been in situations or conditions of similar nature—and having mastered them, they have incorporated the lessons from these experiences into their temperaments. A sister and brother relationship of this nature contributes very much to the family when it is on a high level of evolvement; but when it is on a lower level of evolvement, the family is in a continual state of discord—and there is sorrow for the mother and father.

Souls born into family-atoms come with their treasures or with their burdens. No one single person in the family can bear all of the burdens. Soul-debt burdens are distributed and shared in right timing within the family-atom.

When essential kindness and consideration are not observed, enmities, jealousy, and concealed hatreds are built into a family-atom.

If a religious commitment is absent in the family, the souls embodied therein are inclined toward agnostic, selfish, and materialistic ideals. They produce a condition in the world that feeds not men, but keeps alive the oppositions and force among men.

Today, the one who would serve mankind is faced with a new sort of man coming forth—a new prototype manifesting in the world. This prototype is a man who comes with a prescient mind; he brings aptitudes which have never been known or expressed in the world.

In the family-atom life, the advanced prototypal child produces conditions or situations which have never been known, and less evolved parents find themselves inadequate to cope with the soul-urges of the egos or prototypes born to them. They lack the exegesis to understand such egos.

When a highly evolved child is born into a family-atom already having another child of genius potential, less highly evolved parents are torn in their loyalties. Indescribable pressures are placed upon them; for when exceptional children are born, society begins to intrude more and more into the family. When society begins to intrude into family-atom action, the family-atom loses its virility and vitality. It is only through the spiritual and religious life that the harmony within the family-atom can be sustained. When love and respect between the husband and wife are present, the home is preserved.

Some persons have an aversion to marriage due to environmental restrictions within the family-atom. Children entering the world with marital soul-debts are inclined to be disillusioned as to marriage, due to parental discord. Children born with natural soul-health are uninfluenced by disagreeing parents.

Some persons avoid marriage because they have been celibates in former lives. A spiritual marriage has been consummated within them, and thus they have no need for physical marriage. In the inner spiritual marriage between the spirit and soul, they have made union with the Lord of Love—a union of manifestation, creation.

Enforced celibacy attracts the satanic powers of the dark. When men take upon themselves enforced celibacy, they fall into the pitfalls of lust trials—and an abnormal and unseemly thing occurs.

Some persons who have become impotent due to sexual abuse in this life or in other lives think themselves to be celibate. Unfortunately, lust enters into the lower mind. From impotence, frigidity, and sexual aversion come the malicious gossiper, the maligner of character, and a vulgarity amounting to obsession.

Some persons enter the world knowing themselves to be limited in their sharing. They avoid marriage, even though the opportunity for marriage with many blessings may be offered them. They intuit that they would be inadequate to fulfill the responsibilities of marriage, and therefore prefer to live alone in the world.

Persons who shun marriage because of fear of responsibilities often find themselves with a father, mother, or friend, who places upon their shoulders burdens retrogressive and abnormal to the life-freeing processes.

To feel that marriage is a restraint is to invoke burdens on all levels.

God has ordained that His children shall go forth two by two. If one fails to have a yoke-fellow, the very natural law of balance and equation will attract to him some one or some thing demanding his time, his vitality, his strength, his service, his devotion.

DIVORCE

And the Pharisees came to him, and asked him, Is it lawful for a man to put away his wife: tempting him. And he answered and said unto them, What did Moses command you? And they said, Moses suffered to write a bill of divorcement, and to put her away. And Jesus answered and said unto them, For the hardness of your heart he wrote you this precept.
—St. Mark 10:2-5

During the time of Moses a divorce law was

established which is still active today. Men have heard the words of Jesus as to marriage and as yet are unable to fully adhere to them.

But from the beginning of the creation God made them male and female. For this cause shall a man leave his father and mother, and cleave to his wife; And they twain shall be one flesh: so then they are no more twain, but one flesh. What therefore God hath joined together, let not man put asunder.
—St. Mark 10:6-9

When men begin to evolve into lesser self-genesis, marriage stands forth paramountly on trial. The lesser self-genesis age is the center of chaotic pressures, producing unstable associations and relationships on all levels of human behavior. Morality, fidelity, honor, protection, responsibility—these appear to be empty phrases to egos born into certain family-atoms.

Lesser self-genesis persons are more inclined to divorce than those living on the level of human or family-genesis. A husband and wife expressing lesser self-genesis, both being over-individualistic, are less likely to be charitable and patient with one another. Should there be children or offspring from a former marriage, this will increase the confusion and dissension element within the marriage.

When egos are heavily laden with marital soul-debts from past lives, they cannot sustain a stabilized family-atom action. The result is divorcement. If biological or sexual attraction between marital partners ends—and love has failed to rise with the momentum of sexual affection—the basic affinity nourishing marriage is absent, and division, adultery, neglect, or desertion occurs.

In the lesser self-genesis age, accumulative marital soul-debts are the cause of persons divorcing and remarrying one or more times, for such persons are unable to establish the complete family-atom relationship. These persons, needing companionship, enter into each marriage with a desire for happiness. However, until all accumulative marital soul-debts are erased from the vibratory hum of the soul's medallion, they find it impossible to alter the drifting current of their emotional hungers.

Should a person have the grace to erase all of the accumulative marital soul-debts in one life, he will attract a grace mate in the present life or in the next life, and know a perfect marriage relationship on all levels of affection.

Even though two persons desire to preserve their marriage vows and seek to express the grace side of the marriage, if one or both bring heavy marital debts from past lives, the result is dissension, disagreement, and unhappiness.

Marital soul-debts from former lives are produced by prudery, cupidity, adultery, perversion, precocious celibacy, brutality, irresponsibility, vulgarity, inconstancy, emotional immaturity. These offences against the marriage vow are recorded upon the soul's vibratory hum, and result in accumulative marital soul-debts.

Many egos preparing to enter lesser self-genesis carry heavy marital soul-debts from past lives. These debts are presently being expiated by some through accepting the burden of a loveless marriage or through assuming the burden of divorcement and separation.

Unequal emotional evolvement in marriage produces heavy pressures upon the marriage. Such persons find it impossible to sustain alignment with the higher etheric encasement or grace aspect of a marriage.

When there is incompatibility in a marriage relationship—and divorce occurs—the persons involved may meet in coming lives to balance this unfinished action. However, only in rare instances does one meet and marry again the same person causing marital soul-debts. Absolution of marital soul-debts in coming lives is, as a rule, made possible by an equal situation in marriage. For example, one who has been unfaithful in a former-life marriage will attract an adulterous marital mate in the next life. One who has used cupidity and manipulation in affections, will attract a mate who looks on marriage as a form of possession or ownership.

A person who in a former life has taken a

premature vow of celibacy may find it difficult
to attract a mate—or may attract a mate who is
cold, austere, undemonstrative, insincere. One
who has expressed promiscuity in a former-life
marriage state will attract a mate less mature
in the present life—a mate who sometimes dis-
honors the marriage vows through immorality.
One who has been a prude and frigid as to the
former sexual action in marriage attracts a mate
who is irreverent, over-vulgar, or lustful. One
who has been irresponsible in the stewardship
of joint properties in a former-life marriage is
likely to attract a parasitical mate who defeats
his or her energetic efforts to gain properties
and possessions.

A healthy, reverent marriage love under the
law of God will stimulate those who are married
to love others. Such love is a hospitable love
which in no way lessens the love toward one
another. When one truly loves his mate under
God, it is automatic that he will be more loving, more trusting, more loyal, more reverent to
others in the world.

Christian hospitality may sometimes be felt
by one mate more than the other. A desire to
share one's home and the love emanating therein, when in the heart of but one of the mates,
places restraint upon the family-atom. Hostility
toward other persons is an atavistic reflex un-
natural in a state of healthy marriage. A desire

to share one's hearth in joyous intervals of association is proof of one's soul health and equanimity.

For when they shall rise from the dead, they neither marry, nor are given in marriage; but are as the angels which are in heaven.

—St. Mark 12:25

9

SELF-GENESIS

If one would reach the Holy of Holies, he should sacrifice or relinquish his lower nature. He thus will enter into Aaron's lodge, where he will learn of the shew-bread or the pure prototypes. And he will attain the seven spiritual powers and their resulting authority. He will take into his heart the spiritual essences of God. When the veil between him and the Holy of Holies is lifted, God will speak into his mind through the Word or Logos of the Christ Spirit. And he will become a perfect shewbread or prototype, and will bring forth the spiritual countenance illumined in the Light of God.

The birth of the human spirit extends over many phases and periods covering great aeons of time: the etheric or Edenic; the gravity and physical; the glands and propagation; the tribal; the family; the individual; the world conscience. Men are presently in the process of incorporating the world conscience into the human spirit. When all men are receptive to world conscience, the human spirit will have reached its fulfillment.

When the world conscience is established, humanity and individual man will use the higher virtues of their tribal, racial, family, national, religious, and personal conscience in conjunction with world conscience. The souls of men will be open to one another, and men will live and express their works through the Jesus Ethic. The conscience of man will no longer be burdened by the heavier competitive, prototypal trials. His initiatory experiences will enable him to master the power of imaging, shaping, and forming. If he has a perfectly formed emotional body, and his emotions are in harmony with the divine nuances of love, he will use the power of imaging with ethic, and he will offend not any man.

When men correlate their ethics to the Ethic of Jesus, they will become aware that conscience is a golden heritage inherited from the treasure-house of God. As long as man responds to his conscience, there is hope. Man without conscience is immoral or amoral. When one refuses to respond to his conscience, he invites isolation and ostracism.

An active and stable conscience is necessary that man may live more constructively in family and in society. Society expects man to respond to his conscience, and thereby to abide by the laws of society. True religions and honorable nations also expect man to respond to his conscience.

All decent persons expect man to have a conscience. Where the moral ethos in society is dead, there is perfidy and contempt, for the things of God are absent.

Ideals supporting religions, nations, and families are only as lasting as the purity of the individual conscience. Were this not so, righteous men could neither hear nor respond to the higher ideals of religion, nation, family, and persons.

Standing with man's conscience are two angels—his Guardian Angel and his Recording Angel. These angels, the sentinels of his conscience, remain with him from life to life. They watch over his thoughts and his works. They remind him of the rightness and justice of God's law for him. They also inscribe his guilt upon his waking and sleeping thoughts, that he forget not the good, the true, and the merciful.

When one gives the love of his heart to a person, he feels that the conscience of his beloved will keep watch over their love.

As men evolve, a pure conscience will be more and more valued. Conscience will become the chief asset through which man not only is guided, but through which other men respect him and trust him. When men have attained a *prescient conscience,* they will have entered the state of higher self-genesis.

A good conscience is the watchman over good

and evil. Evil conscience encourages evil inclination, and results in flagrant disobedience of law. Prescient conscience is supreme good in action.

To recognize the sovereign right of each individual to unite with his personal conscience; with the conscience of his tribe, race, family, nation; and with the world conscience—is to acknowledge the dignity of each soul in the earth.

An ethical person is more sensitive to the world conscience. He can know neither contentment nor peace in his heart and mind unless he is peacefully united with his fellow man. The sorrows of the world weigh upon the heart with a purging intensity in one who would serve his fellow man—for in serving his fellow man he serves God.

A darkened tribal conscience produces cannibalism, superstitions, incest, sterility, and decadence. A heavily weighted family conscience causes the family to become indolent, immoral, unreliable, belligerent, unsympathetic, irreverent, unfaithful.

If religious conscience is absent in a body of worship, the Holy Ghost absents Himself; the mystical body of the church worship becomes sterile, vacuous—and, finally, dies. Persecution, bigotry, and agnosticism result.

An imbalanced national conscience incites

revolution; atheism becomes predominant. Decaying, amoral actions are common. Homosexuality, graft, unjust legal pressures, lack of charity, neglect of the masses, and unjust, partial leadership are prevalent.

If one chooses to seal away his personal conscience, a criminal mind is developed. Lust, greed, and envy make a mockery of human dignity and self respect.

A lesser self-genesis person who is disobedient to the voice of conscience expresses self-deception, dishonesty, unreliability, amorality, agnosticism, egotism, and frenzied inconstancies.

In lesser self-genesis, man is concerned solely with consciousness; self-awareness predominates over conscience. The conscience of a lesser self-genesis man must speak to him through subtle or indirect ways. One who deliberately turns away from responding to his conscience—because he feels that he is submitting his will to traditional concepts—experiences dreams which are heavily laden with reminders from his conscience. Through dreams his Guardian Angel sees that he is ever reminded of wrongdoing.

The mental and emotional suffering in lesser self-genesis is more intense than in any other genesis. When men suffer in tribal-genesis, they have the protection of the communal conscience overdirecting the tribe. When men suffer in family-genesis, they have the sympathy and the empathy within the family-atom; the conscience of the family is always present to remind the one suffering that he has in some manner disobeyed certain rules of the body or certain ethics of conduct or certain Laws of God.

Suffering and conscience are linked together; they are twin actions. If man fails to respond to his conscience and its disciplining action, he suffers; thus, all sicknesses are tied in with a feeling of having neglected one's conscience.

The lesser self-genesis man depends more on what he experiences and what he thinks he knows. He is contemptuous of tender approaches to his soul, and he is blind to the laws of righteousness existing in the world. He is often cynical—and distrustful of others. He is prone to blame or to put the burden of his mistakes on others, as he is deaf to the voice of his conscience.

The lesser self-genesis person has much of the Lucifer Angels in his nature. He is prideful; he is in love with himself. He often procrastinates in his better nature of hospitality and of love. He is either partially loving, or he is lustfully loving, or possessively loving.

The lesser self-genesis man thinks that conscience is the product of various disciplines by traditional bodies—religious, parental, and collectively national on various levels. He does not know that conscience is a spiritual asset to which he has access, and by which he may guide his ship and come safely home.

As men become more egotistical in lesser self-genesis, they receive ego-shattering lessons that return them to their conscience. On awakening to the conscience, one dies to egotism. Very often there are many tears of self-reproach and states of melancholy; there is much grieving, and the revealing of dimensions of selfishness in one's nature. This is a period of dying to the *egotistical shell*.

If over many lives one has failed to respond to tribal conscience, family conscience, and to his own conscience, he has built around him an egotistical shell. This shell is a heavy, clouded atmosphere surrounding his complete body and particularly his heart and mind. The egotistical shell produces a form of conscience-claustrophobia.

When the egotistical shell has reached its most hardened state, an interior fire begins. This fire produces inner pain, self-searching, and finally, the discovery of oneself.

In the latter stages of the egotistical shell's dissolving, one loses his sense of humor, especially his sense of humor regarding himself. He interprets everything seriously; he feels burdened and weighted down. He does not understand the spiritual powers of his soul. He has yet to confirm the association of the Holy Presences in Mediation.

The dissolving of the egotistical shell continues over a period of time until finally one surrenders his self-will. His self-consciousness then comes under the direction of a higher degree of conscience, called prescient conscience. When one achieves prescient conscience, he stands under the Law of God; he assumes full responsibility for his own actions. He sees God in man's world as being the supreme motivating Will.

Animals living in the environment of tribes take on something of the tribal conscience; they learn to protect the tribe, and they are violently suspicious of those who are not of the tribe.

Animals associated with a family as household pets or companions are influenced by the conscience of the family. If the family be brutish, the animal is brutish; if the family is selfish, the animal is destructive. This is also true with children in tribes and children in families.

In lesser self-genesis, domestic pets or animals take on the appearance of their masters. When the conscience does not speak through a person in lesser self-genesis, it often speaks through the animal; the animal may become sick, in that it must bear the brunt of an imbalanced conscience of an individual who is its master or owner. The neurotic weaknesses of a pampered animal are caused by the selfishness of an emotionally immature master.

This also pertains to children. Children who are the offspring of emotionally immature lesser self-genesis persons sense that they cannot rely upon the conscience of their parents. Such children become over-precocious, compensating for their feelings of insecurity. When a child loses moral contact with the conscience attribute of the family, he has no guide to gauge right or wrong. Such children need to be trained as to ethics.

When conscience is awakened in a lesser self-genesis person, it is often difficult for him to transmit to his children his new set of values. He finds it difficult to communicate with his children as a responsible parent, or to communicate with them as a person. This is a tragic situation, in which not only the parent suffers but also the family and the children.

Conscience affects persons contacting one another in friendship. Friendship is a healthy relationship between persons when each one has a stable conscience. When one is attracted to a friend who is approaching the state of having conscience, he should respond to him in a most dear and intimate way. These friendships and associations may become resourceful and lasting. It is unfortunate that in lesser self-genesis, when men are without conscience, friendships are rarely lasting. There are always restraints or barriers between such persons.

To live in lesser self-genesis, devoid of a full and active conscience, is an unhappy and bitter life—a most lonely and desolate life. Regardless of how much culture one has attained, or regardless of his refinement in association, one without conscience is always seeking something more. His true hunger is for constancy in friendship and association.

When egotism is transformed into humility, one acknowledges that God governs the universe, and that God alone holds the answer to his desolateness. He holds up his conscience to God, and God revives it. His soul-powers become active; he begins to move freely between the lesser and the higher promptings of his conscience. He begins to understand when a "no" means "no." He also begins to understand when a "yes, yes, yes" means "yes."

In lesser self-genesis, choice and will have more free play than in any other degree of genesis. Therefore, lesser self-genesis is a painful state; it is, however, a necessary stage in evolvement. God set man free with choice and with a certain degree of will. God gave the conscience to be the watchtower and the watchman over man's will. When one understands that self-will is nothing unless it is immersed in God's Will, then his angel comes forth and he begins to receive holy guidance—which works directly with his conscience. His conscience becomes prescient conscience, and he has reached the state of higher self-genesis.

Initiations into true charitableness begin when one places his hand in the hand of his angel and saith unto him, "I would serve."

Unto the pure all things are pure; but unto them that are defiled and unbelieving is nothing pure; but even their mind and conscience is defiled.

—Titus 1:15

Self-genesis is divided into two parts. The first part of self-genesis is for the purpose of producing individuality; the second part of self-genesis is for the purpose of producing selflessness. Whereas personality is produced from tribal and family association, individuality is produced from associating with persons outside the tribe or family. The unfamiliar and non-blood relatings work to produce individuality for man.

In the first part of self-genesis, an individualistic atom begins to manifest in man's mental body, and he develops a positive and strong individuality. He becomes emotionally detached from the former family encasement, and seeks to blend with society rather than with family. In this, he loses the close, intimate love he formerly had for his family association. His energies move into the thought world; his emotions are muted and inarticulate. The intellect being predominant, he becomes more critical in his attitude toward love and its demands upon him. He expresses wrong expectations toward love, expecting to be loved despite his critical mind and selfish actions. In his desire for individuality, he fails to fulfill the expectations of others. He develops strong guilt feelings due to certain unfulfilled family relationships, and a tremendous strain is placed upon the mental body, endangering his mental health.

In lesser self-genesis, one works with the talents he brings from many former lives. He strives, through individuality, to fulfill perfection in talent. He relies solely upon his egotism, and trusts only his intellect. He worships his own intellect, as his intellect is his God.

The lesser self-genesis person seeks to bring forth an individualistic atom in the mental body. In this, he expresses a strong individuality and, in some rare instances, genius. Because he is encased in an egotistical shell, and is yet to bring forth pure love, his danger is personalized egotism, self-aggrandizement, and the basking in self-acclaim and self-love.

His consciousness is colored by a war between

logic and a hidden hunger for love. As he approaches higher degrees of self-genesis, he suffers certain humiliations, demotions of pride, that he may dissolve his egotistical shell, and balance his thoughts with love. He is, in reality, seeking to find an ethic, and therefore prepare himself for the latter stages of self-genesis, in which he will express pure ethics. He begins to see God as The Intelligence and The Plan.

In one of the early phases of self-genesis, man's ideal is preservation of his right to think and act as an individual, and his right to explore every degree of life. From this phase of self-genesis has come the scientific age.

In certain earlier stages of self-genesis, there is a period in which man's temperament swings completely to the opposite of reverence. Thus, he expresses irreverence for the proven things of the past. He attacks, and becomes antagonistic to, the decaying ideals centered in family or tribe. He seeks, intellectually, to preserve the ideal in self-discovery and experience. Irreverence and intellect become the critical mind. He despises historical inheritance, both religious and educational. He fortifies himself only through self-opinion—and he would lay to waste everything which has formerly produced the cultures of mankind. From this come revolutions in governments, separateness in families, upheavals in religions; and unreasoning prejudices against races, creeds, and religions are accentuated.

As one gradually evolves in self-genesis, his irreverence begins to be rationalized through certain fundamental laws; and the supporting truths of the universe become apparent to the higher logic within his thought world. The violent, hidden or open rebellion against tradition and its inheritance is tempered into a higher phase of reasoning, accompanied by a degree of reverence for the worthwhile attributes of man as to feeling and thinking. Out of this come the higher phases of self-genesis. Persons in higher self-genesis preserve the ideals which present to man his right to feel reverent, to love selflessly, and to worship and find God.

In the second part of self-genesis, one desires to teach and impart instruction, showing what the ideal man can be—so that others in the world, in their relating to God, may seek to become the *ideal man.*

In the last part of self-genesis, one strives for impersonality rather than personality. His senses become soul-faculties. He uses the higher degrees of emotion and thought. And he strives for selfless serving and dedication, so that in the coming genesis, cosmos-genesis, he may become a Being, and express through unobstructed Mediation in alignment with the Christ Mind.

In higher self-genesis, the conflict and sepa-

rateness within the family group are replaced
by honoring and respecting the individuality
of each member of the family. Love is expressed
on a higher spiral. Such families consist of purer
egos who, as catalyst associates, create within
the rising spiral of evolutionary cultures.

In lesser self-genesis, one begins his work of
self-discovery. In this, there is an accentuation
of self-centeredness. Jesus, the most selfless
being ever to live in the world, taught men to
deny themselves and to take up their cross and
follow Him. In higher self-genesis, one learns
to recognize the difference between conceit and
selflessness. Humility and self-denial give him
the means of freeing his true being, given of
God. The higher self-genesis person channels
his works, emotions, and intellect into a pur-
poseful and spiritual life.

In the present age of birth to lesser self-genesis, the mental and emotional neuroses and the
unpredictable amoral acts are caused by extreme internal pressures; the initiatory trials
through emotions and mentality are accelerated.
The world conscience, the family-atom conscience, and the individual conscience press
heavily upon those who have been laggard in
responding to the spiritual laws ruling the
universe.

The Old Testament is a true record of the
transition process of man's rise from tribal-

genesis to human-genesis. The New Testament contains the promise of man's spiritual potential in self-genesis, cosmos-genesis, and pro-genesis.

In lesser self-genesis, one receives help from the Recording Angel and the Guardian Angel of the family-atom when he holds sacred the family relationship. When a person in lesser self-genesis becomes free of his egotistical shell, he receives direct help from his personal angels—and, sometimes, he begins to be aware of his personal angels.

When a person achieves higher self-genesis, he is constantly aware of the presence of his angels and their ministering helps. And he begins to align himself with the Kingdoms of Angels and their work with the world.

The higher self-genesis person seeks to channel his spiritual gifts, so that he may selflessly work as a world-server to overcome world-karma. In his seeking to serve, he is confronted with his unresolved karma of tribal-genesis, family-genesis, and lesser self-genesis. From this come frequent dweller experiences, presenting to him certain degrees of opposition or karmic contest in his rise to a spiritual life. These challenges may be presented from race, family, nation, society, religion—or from his personal soul-debts of the past.

A person in higher self-genesis achieves soul-powers and frees his higher levels of grace. He begins to use the spiritual gifts gathered from aeons of living in this eternity, and he gains the ethic through which he may serve.

The higher self-genesis man becomes at one with the experiences of mankind. He works selflessly, and dedicates to the Eternals, that he may think through the Christ Mind, and thus heal, serve, instruct, and teach through the greater archetypes and Will in God.

In self-genesis, reincarnation is accelerated, and one moves more quickly from life to life. In the latter part of self-genesis, a dedicated person who is uniquely suited for certain tasks may, previous to birth, choose his future sex, environment, and vocation.

In all phases of self-genesis, karma moves at a very rapid pace—and there is instantaneous reproving as to one's feelings, thoughts, and actions. In the latter part of self-genesis, one's karmic labors and responsibilities are heavy, in that he must incorporate certain karma from former genesis levels. Karma is clearly perceived by him; he recognizes eternity justice. His goal is set upon a life of dedication and selfless serving.

Since the coming of Jesus, man has begun, through the aid of the Christ-Light, to command the etheric compulsions of the world-soul atom, the survival compulsions of the tribal-atoms, and the personality compulsions of the family-atoms—so that he may begin to experience the impulse of a spiritual life, and thus become part of a greater body of Mediation working with the Lord Christ, the Son of God.

When man is no longer subjected to the great over-atom compulsions in tribal-genesis and family-genesis, and the first impulses of individuality in self-genesis, he begins to rely solely upon his own atom evolvement and alignment with the Christ. The degree of his alignment and dedication to the Christ Spirit directs him to an association with spiritual persons who reflect the twelve disciples accompanying the Lord Jesus—the twelve disciples of Jesus being the raised aspect of the twelve tribes of Jacob.

In the latter part of self-genesis, one comes closer to the Christ-impulse, and thus becomes penetrable to the honeycomb filigree action in Mediation. Thereafter, he begins his true expression and is at home in the physical world as well as in the Spiritual World.

When men of virtue and ethic achieve cosmos-genesis, they will come under Divine Spirit. They will have absorbed all that the earth has to offer them. Such men will be ready to come under the instruction of Divine Spirit—the Christ.

Divine-Spirit man of the earth will have been born through struggle, sorrow, pain. The pain octave of the earth which has pressed upon him—that he might know the degrees of feeling between extreme pain and extreme joy—will cease its pressure.

In cosmos-genesis, the pain octave in the earth will be experienced only by those who have refused to respond to the Light. Their suffering will be not as men know suffering in this time; it will be a mental anguish, a desolate aloneness of spirit.

Cosmos-genesis is the time when "the sheep and the goats" will be separated. The goats are the Cains of the world—the takers and the tyrants of the world.

When Divine Spirit is established in this earth, all laggard souls will enter into a twilight state of sleep and will prepare for the ending of this eternity. The dark angel, Lucifer, who watches over the darkened outer sphere, will consummate his work; and, in the last Great Interval of this eternity system, will assist all laggard souls to prepare to enter into eternity systems where they may begin again.

In pro-genesis, men will be manifestors, having earned the Melchizedek powers—the power to increase and the power to decrease. Their thoughts will be scintillating manifestors for God. Pro-genesis souls will work directly with the archetypes to be used when this earth has begun again a new eternity day.

Even as Hierarchy, in the great zodiacal system, knows total harmony in Mediation, so will pro-genesis men work together. Opposition, competition and antagonism will be unknown. ". . . there shall be no death, neither sorrow, nor crying, neither shall there be any more pain: for the former things are passed away." (Revelations 21:4)

In pro-genesis, man will be similar to the angels, as the substance of his body will be translucent, incorruptible. As the stars sang together in Job's description, so shall the pro-genesis souls sing the creative word with joy.

In the next genesis, all-genesis, men will work in a perfected imaging action. In this, Mediation will reach its uttermost creative tone.

In the last and final genesis of this eternity, called one-genesis, all who are to be born into other eternity systems will enter into a cosmic sleep. The Omega-tones will sound. The substance of the earth, having changed, will be transformed once more into a fiery body similar to the sun.

The meek, who are to work with hierarchy powers in the beginning of the new eternity day for the earth, will remain conscious. They will witness the ending of this eternity, and record it in their minds. Their bodies of Light will be of such fine consistency that the physical fire of the earth will touch them not.

10

INITIATION

Men now prepare to know more of Jesus and to live by His Ethic. They will begin first by returning to the early Apostle powers of healing, of ministering to the sick, and of consummating holy miracles or anastasis feats for the body, mind, and soul.

There exists in the world today a handful of God. They are the true spiritual healers. On the crest of human need, some of these healers will gradually open the portals to the eternals through the undertsanding of their fellow man.

Through human urgencies and emergencies and crises, healers will come forth— healers who will pattern their techniques after the formulas of Jesus.

THE OCTAVE OF PAIN

Men who choose darkness rather than light choose suffering. Suffering is the result of unknowing. Those who are inwardly true to the guidance of the Spirit of God in their souls— and to the mediation of His angels—are the hope of the world. The skills of their souls become pointers toward the needs of humankind. Their healing talents and their perspective into the suffering of other men enable them to alleviate the suffering in the world.

When the Word of God sounded in the beginning of this eternity, there were thirteen differentiated creative tones within the Word. When the planet Saturn was projected into its orbit around the sun, the eighth tone of creation became the octave tone of pain. This pain octave is centered in the inner core of the earth, and works with the axis of the earth. As long as this octave sounds, men will live through the alternates of joy and sorrow, pain and health, peace and dissension, love and hate.

In the earth no one is completely exempt from pain. Even the Lord Jesus suffered pain—that He might lift the world. Men suffer pain—that they might lift themselves. For long eras of eternity time they have wandered in labyrinths of trial and error. Each time a person concludes a trial-and-error initiation with victory, he has mastered something of the Saturn lower octave of pain.

At the time of the resurrection of Jesus, the Christ Spirit took command of the axis of the earth. Man began to receive the greater nuances within the creative tones through the mediation of the Christ Spirit or Son of God.

When men fulfill the Jesus Ethic, the octave of pain will cease to play upon their hearts, minds, and wills. Through the use of the Jesus Ethic, men will move beyond the alternates of joy and sorrow into a holy joy. They will know an immortal health—and their well-being will give health to those who suffer. The peace in their hearts and minds will extinguish the fiery dissensions in the world. Their spiritual love will mitigate hate among men. The higher aspect of the eighth tone in the creative Word will be heard by reverent men, and they will respond to the eternal vitality within their wills, thoughts, emotions, and works. They will act toward their fellow men with mercy, compassion, and love.

The alternate-trials of suffering and health experienced over the ages and aeons will produce a victorious man or a perfected man who will use his skills as an impassioned creator for God. Through billions of years of overcoming, this will be made possible.

Jesus of Nazareth came to the world as a Healer and a Saviour, that man might receive the lifting, overcoming, and resurrection powers—and thus rise over the eighth-octave alternate trials.

Pure healers and all spiritually mediative persons are aware of the overcoming powers. Persons yet to be initiated into their rational minds are unaware of the importance of the alternates existing in the world. They see suffering and pain in the world and have not the answer to the cause, the reason, or the why of pain.

Spiritual healers who are aware of the souls of men have undergone the baptismal initiatory trials of blood, water, fire, and light. These are the rational healers in the world who understand why wars come, why men suffer, why some are born deformed, mentally infirm, or less evolved than others. They see these painful repetitive events and conditions as the result of a supreme or eternal justice. Such healers work to see the cause, to comprehend it, and to heal its effect mediatively, without judgment.

Those who walk the spiritual path know that their mental, emotional, and spiritual attitudes are sounding harps through which God speaks to other men. Their responsibility is inestimable. To vary from ethic not only invites peril to their souls, but sets up a dissonance in the human spirit—affecting and reverberating upon the souls of all men.

There are periods when the lower tone of the eighth octave sounds more disastrously upon men. This occurs when God, His Hierarchs and angels add impetus to the tone of creation. When men fall into complacency, they attract the destroying tone of the eighth octave. The agitation of the pain octave seeks to re-shape and re-mold men, that their weaknesses may be translated into spiritual strengths, and their strengths into spiritual power.

Through the great alternates, man will gradually develop a consciousness having assets and attributes extending beyond the consciousness he had on entering this eternity system. To achieve command of the alternates has been the work of all persons since the beginning of their falling from the etheric state into the gravity state of living and being.

When God willed this eternity system into being, He sounded the Alpha-tones of His creative Word into the sacred atoms of all living things. When the lower octave of pain is accelerated within the earth, it is felt upon the sacred atom within the heart of man.

In his heart, in his love, man is initiated first into the love of those nearest him. He is next initiated into the love of those associated with him as neighbors, friends, society, humanity. Until he has opened completely the sympathy buds of his heart, he will be confused and incomplete; he will experience the negative side of the alternates, and he will know long and painful periods of desolateness.

The Spirit of God teaches man of love first through his fellow man. Only when man effortlessly and naturally coordinates his love of persons with his love of God may he be said to have fulfilled the total heart initiations.

The mass struggle now being experienced in the world is due to the intensified pressures of the destroying aspect of the eighth octave of pain. These unhappy events occur so that men may be purged and made more sincere in their motive and intent, more truthful, honest, and teachable.

The older moral laws will be reborn in those less evolved. The Jesus Ethic will be applied by souls who are united with the creative healing aspect commanding the eighth octave of pain. Jesus said, "Behold, I give unto you power to tread on serpents and scorpions, and over all the power of the enemy: and nothing shall by any means hurt you." (St. Luke 10:19)

The human-spirit heart will be a heart consisting wholly of charity and mercy toward one's fellow man; mercy balanced with spiritual insight into the interior causes of pain and suffering; mercy supreme over condemnation and judgment.

INITIATION

That thou might heal thy bones, go to trees. That thou might heal thy lungs, go to trees. That thou might heal thy thoughts and lift them to high places, go thou to trees.

When thou wouldst heal the aeon memories,

go to mountains. When thou wouldst heal the secrets in thyself and become selfless, go thou to mountains.

And when thou wouldst be purified in thy lesser self and thou wouldst be cleansed in thy emotions, go thou to the waters.

All men in the earth are in an incessant state of initiation. Throughout the ages they have entered into the gates of instruction or knowledge through initiation. From initiation, men learn and change. It is God's Will that men be initiated. Through initiation, they are changed and transformed. Birth, sorrow, loss, lack, pain, suffering, and death are initiations.

When men were first encased in tribes, they experienced initiations through initiatory rituals set down by the tribal chief and priest. They were initiated into the use of the fiery ether within the plant world. They were also initiated into the organic or mineral life of the earth. Through initiations they learned the secrets of the mineral and etheric fires in rocks, stones, and ores. From this they produced fire with which to warm themselves and to cook their food. They were also initiated into the sentient moods existing in the animal kingdom. Finally they were initiated into the sexual taboos, from which they learned of their ancestral origins and the ties of blood. They united with the Propagation Angels of the tribes and learned of conception and birth, the care of children, and the preserving of sexual purity in the tribe.

When men moved into the earlier phases of human-genesis or family-atom action, they came under seven initiations: sexual selection, self-denial, faith, affection, true words, reverence for good, trust in God.

When an ego fails to use what he has been taught through the sexual initiations in the tribal and family-atom, he must undergo, over long periods of time, initiation into the sacredness of sex. If one has retained lust in his sexual nature; if he is prudish or fearful in his sexual attitudes; or if he seeks out irreverent and unworthy persons to share his sexual life—the Angels of Chastity will scourge him, until he has reached a period of self-loathing and desires with his total being to live a chaste life.

In the family-atom action, various members of the family are used to challenge one's giving and sharing. Until one learns self-denial, he will continue to be challenged by brothers and sisters, or father or mother. Society will also place upon him work-burdens for which he receives neither credit nor reward.

In the latter phases of human-genesis, one comes face to face with the need to receive from God a reassurance of His Being. He is initiated into seven tone levels of faith: faith in a loved one; faith in the justice of things as they are; faith in God's Supreme care of him; faith in the Love of God animating all souls; faith in one's own self-esteem and worth; faith in the Light and its works; faith in one's own spiritual power. Every level of these initiations is experienced to some degree in family-atom action.

As one enters the first phases of lesser self-genesis, his individuality is more accentuated, and he often loses touch with his higher intuition and his faith. To him, his individuality and self-importance are foremost. Being devoid of the naive ideals he formerly had, he feels and thinks through a materialistic image—he thinks upon what is due him, rather than what he can do for others. His sexual life is one of experiment and exploring. He expects others to give to him. He knows little of sacrifice. He is uncomfortable when the soul is mentioned, as he thinks that belief in a soul places him into a dependent meekness unsuitable to him. In his conversation, he is sarcastic, curt, caustic, often twisting words to gain his ends. He sees other men through the eye of cynicism. He looks upon them as "suckers." And, if they are more successful than he, he is envious of their "luck." He has forgotten there is spiritual power, and he is allergic to spiritual persons.

The lesser self-genesis person, lacking reverence and faith, produces a materialistic age. His body, his emotions, and his soul are subjected to a life of force, hate, and pressure. When the initiations of lesser self-genesis are concluded, one enters into a certain austerity affecting the sexual life. He learns to love again and to see the sexual act as a sacred, reverent action. In his appetites and habits he practices self-denial. He gradually learns to release possessions, persons, and self-will.

The initiation into faith, for the higher self-genesis mind, is a rapturous experience; it is also an emotionally and mentally painful experience, as he must unite with his Recording Angel and rectify past calloused actions and deeds.

The higher self-genesis initiate expresses purity in sex, self-denial. He has absolute faith in the Will of God. He loves his fellow man and those near him who share his love. He encourages men and inspires them through his healing words of love. He thinks with an illumined mind, seeing always God as the Creator, as the One.

It is God's Will that man shall have honor, substance, loving relationships, and health of the body, emotions, mind, and soul. Man earns these through initiation. He undergoes initiation that he may gain these in the world—and more, that he may gather a higher degree of consciousness and become at one with the Christ Mind.

There are many and varied degrees of initiation, but there are four supporting themes in all initiatory experience:

Sickness of the body, that one may be purified and cleansed. One gains the benefit of sickness initiation when he learns that each sickness contains a way to attain a greater degree of consciousness.

One who is without possessions is being taught the ethic of stewardship.

One who is dishonored, slandered or vilified is being taught to honor other men, and thereby to honor his Father which art in Heaven.

To suffer through family, marriage, children, brothers, sisters, or any blood-tie relationship, is to be initiated into kinship in life, and thus to be prepared to fulfill the human-spirit ideal as given of God.

The Biblical drama of Job is a prototypal initiation story portraying higher family-atom initiation and lesser self-genesis initiation. Job's complacency is a common fault and a snare experienced by many persons. When such persons come under the higher command of their souls, they are ready to widen the horizons of their understanding, and thus they undergo initiation to purge them of any flaws in their character and temperament.

Job believed in God, but his faith had become static. His engrossment and pride in his family, in his possessions, in the praises of other men stood between him and God. He took for granted his good health, and he thought it his just due to have possessions. He forgot that his grace had earned him his honor. He forgot that God had sent his children to him and could also recall them.

When Job reached the time of utter self-satisfaction, he was ripe for Satan to search him and to assess him. In the purifying fires of retrospection, Job experienced the challenges and trials which an initiate must undergo. His three comfortless comforters represented three sides of the nature to which he was dying. These comforters made it possible for him to make lucid his thinking and to spiritually rationalize his true relationship with God.

Each one in the world, if he would rise, must place his mind upon the reality of God, rather than upon what is speaking in the world.

Smugness is a cardinal sin in the spiritual life. And spiritual pride must die when one would be used by God to do greater things.

After Job lost his possessions, suffered the most degrading of sicknesses, had his children taken from him through death, and his friends deserted him—forgetting his great humanitarian ways—Job was emptied out, that God might

fill him anew with living verities closer to his
soul's intent. All initiates must be emptied out,
that they may be filled with the true waters of
life.

When a person is found worthy to serve God,
he must loose his hold upon all things material
and temporal, and lean solely upon lasting and
eternal spiritual values.

Job was demoted that he might see God as
the Giver of all things, and himself as but the
steward of honor, health, family, and possessions. Job suffered abasement and mortification
that he might value what God had given him.

Jesus' parable of the talents parallels the prototypal story of Job. Piety and total engrossment in the world do not feed the soul. Worship of God is a vital thread or artery, and is
kept alive only by a continuing remembrance
that Eternal Spirit is the Will and the Life.

Job is the example of a person who has great
spiritual potential, and has access to all of the
good things in the physical world, accepting
them as his right, and thinking that he alone
has earned them. When one experiences the Job
initiatory trials, his initiation is to observe the
ethic in the use of his honor and good name;
to reverently use his body; and to appreciate the
treasures of life-giving, life-restoring health.
Through initiation he learns to use possessions
with ethic; he becomes willing to earn and to

give of himself to his work, that he may be a craftsman under the authority of God.

The true healing of complacency comes when one is grateful to God that men think highly of him, that men esteem him and respect him. When one is grateful for the health of his body, his cells and his blood become spiritually sweet; he balances the antagonisms among the bacteria in his body. When he is grateful for his family, for their love, and is tender and forgiving to those who are related to him by blood, he will earn higher family relationships. Spiritual strength will give him insight into all human weaknesses. Human ties will become more flexible through forgiveness, pity, and compassion.

When one is grateful for his possessions, he is spiritually rich in the good things over which he is steward. When other men know famine, he feeds them from the storehouse of his own riches.

The person who undergoes more than one Job initiatory trial in one life is blessed, for he is preparing to render greater service for God.

The human spirit, in its present work of changing and transforming, expresses itself more prominently in the man of mercy and compassion. God is using men of mercy to inspire other men to rise, to give them hope, to heal their fears, and to open the rivers of peace conjoining the hearts of all men. Men of mercy in this climactic era are few. In tribes, races, nations, and families, those having the most sensitive awareness of the needs of the world are now undergoing initiatory trials, that they may become healing mediators. All men are potential mediative healers of other men. Merciful, charitable souls in the human family are opening their vision, that they may look into the hearts of other men.

There is only one way the mediator-initiate can maintain his poise in these crucial times: he must come under the Jesus Ethic. Through the use of the Jesus Ethic, his insight and his perception will be magnified, and the suffering of the peoples of the earth will be mirrored to him. His one purpose will be to find a way to equip himself to serve. God will hear his cry, and will use him.

The most remembered works of Jesus are His healing miracles. The spiritually initiated now work to come under the Jesus Ethic. Through the use of the Jesus Ethic, they will attain liberty for their souls, and thus give ease to the suffering in the world.

There are many ways through which men may be healed, and through which the Jesus Ethic is manifested. The Lord Jesus is the true Physician. He is the restoring Artery between man and our Father which art in Heaven.

Medical science, intensifying its research into

the organism and intricate functions of the physical body of man, will expand its techniques and skills—giving remedy, care, ease, and release from sickness. Medical science will respond to other sciences. The sciences of energies in foods, in minerals, in the sun, in the plants will be incorporated into the science of medicine.

As the etheric encasements encompassing tribes, races, nations, and families are loosened and opened, bacteria heretofore dormant in man's physical system will be activated. Diseases will appear which are presently unknown to medical science.

Physicians who work with the higher ethic of their souls and the merciful attributes within their natures will be given new therapies and remedies with which to give ease to the suffering masses. Such physicians will recognize the spiritual laws supporting healing.

The therapeutic arts which have been so long neglected will be used in the new medicine by dedicated physicians. There will be less division among physicians. Medical science will be more concerned with the cause of suffering than with the appearance defining suffering, and therefore will call upon other sciences for assistance.

The spiritual person is being initiated that he may make himself at one with the need of races, nations, families and persons. The emotional convulsions now active in the world are experienced to some degree by the initiate in his inner life, as well as in his outer life.

True mediative healing begins with selfless prayer. Prayer sent forth by a merciful heart will result in acts of manifold mercy.

One who would spiritually serve his brother must be free of a condemning and judging mind. The techniques of mediative healing may be used successfully only by a forgiving and non-judging person.

When a person prays for one man, he is praying for all men. And when healing comes as a result of his prayer, there is a greater degree of harmony for the human spirit as a whole.

All forms of healing, physical or spiritual, are mediative. However, no healing is possible when the sacred atom of the heart and the pulsation of the soul are separated by lack of faith. The sacred atom of the heart contains the restoring-life sealed into all men by the Father since the beginning of this eternity. When one offends the sacred atom of the heart by offensive and self-willed actions; when one abuses love, or follows shallow intellectual pursuits—the sacred atom of the heart, and the restoring-life dwelling therein, fail to give forth the renewing and regenerating vitality. Illness, sickness, and discomfort are the result.

To repent of wrongdoing, selfish feelings,

and unjust thoughts—and to surrender one's egotistical will to the Will of God—transforms transitory beliefs into an immovable faith in the healing powers of God.

All sicknesses are initiatory trials. In each sickness, there is a reason and a cause. In an initiatory trial, one may see the reason for his sickness, but he may not yet be able to cope with the cause. When he is spiritually competent to understand the cause, he will be shown a way to set aright the cause. As long as he is dependent upon his transitory beliefs rather than faith, he will understand only the surface reason for his sickness. However, in time, as he evolves through prayer and continued faith, he shall have the cause revealed to him by his Recording Angel.

Beliefs are steppingstones across the river of life. Whatever one believes, he will receive. One may have many beliefs. These may lead him into false or faulty ways; but if he has unwavering faith, he cannot be lost, nor can he be separated from God.

Faith is an eternal attribute. Belief is but an offshoot of faith, and is a temporary means through which man experiences, explores, and learns. Beliefs, being transitory, can be colored by doubt. When there is perfect faith, one may do the things Jesus promised in St. Matthew 21:21—

Verily I say unto you, If ye have faith, and doubt not, ye shall not only do this which is done to the fig tree, but also if ye shall say unto this mountain, Be thou removed, and be thou cast into the sea; it shall be done.

When one has faith "as a grain of mustard seed," he will receive a healing grace from the higher powers of Mediation. Such faith enables one to receive a permanent healing. When one has faith, he enters into the greatest mediative arteries of God. Faith enables the heavenly helps of Mediation to manifest their perfect works, and thus unite the sufferer with the restoring life sealed into the sacred atom of the heart by "our Father which art in Heaven."

Wherever there is pain, there is some form of imbalance. The more one desires to bring harmony to his life, and balance to his works, the more sensitive he will become. He will gain this sensitivity through discomfort and pain in the human body, disturbed or famished emotions, anguish and anxiety in thought, and the weightedness one assumes when he aids the Lord Jesus to lift the burdens in the world.

For every pain, God has given a remedy. For all suffering, God has given stamina and compensation. For all sorrow, God has given comfort and wisdom. If one will obey and listen to the Will of God, the mercy of God will send a way of release from pain. Reverent prayer and sustained faith will inevitably disclose the lesson within sickness.

Only one Being has lived in the earth with a perfect body, perfect emotions, and a perfect mind. This was the Lord Jesus. When men are like Jesus, there shall be no human ailments and no physical deformities in the world. Because men are yet learning, there will continue to be ailments of the human body. Such ailments are the result of man's unknowing—which waits to be resolved through the soul's timing and action.

Through prayer and faith, a person may so raise his degree of light that the very cells of his body may be filled with a heavenly vibrancy. It is the work of the Mediative Healer to help the sick to sustain this Light.

When the Mediative Healer prays for a person, the person will respond to his prayers by being attracted to one or more of the mediative plateaus of healing. The person's degree of belief and depth of faith, working with his soul-debt and soul-grace, will determine the manner in which his relief or healing will come. If he has some soul-debt yet unresolved, and some lesson to learn, he will receive temporary relief. If the soul-debt is resolved, he will receive a permanent healing.

There are seven mediative plateaus of healing in the physical world:

I. *Walking and exercise for the body*

To rejuvenate the circulation and the blood stream.

To bring the respiratory system and muscular system into harmony.

To return one to a mediative alignment with Nature and its virginal helps.

II. *Massage and corrective therapy for the skeletal structure*

A person led to this mediative plateau of healing should pray to be led to a dedicated healer, so as to avoid the dangers of mesmeric magnetism and hypnotic suggestion sometimes used in physical contact therapies.

III. *Eating and food-chemistry*

Through guidance one will discover his personal rhythms for eating and the foods best suited to his individual chemistry. He will seek vital foods. Devitalized, denatured, gross foods will be avoided. All foods from which the life-germ has been removed will be offensive to his digestion and will imbalance the nutrition within the body.

IV. *Natural, herbal medications*

Through natural, herbal medications, he will seek to energize and give vitality to his body.

V. *Medicine and surgery*

Through medicine and surgery, he will place his dependence upon the ethical diagnosis, physical ministrations, and skills of a qualified and dedicated physician.

VI. *Correction of the emotions and thoughts*
Through self-searching and a desire for self-discovery, he will find a way to correct his immature emotions and thoughts.

VII. *The Mediative Healer*
His angels will direct him to a Mediative Healer who will open the door to the Healing Ministry of Heaven.

God is in all substances. He is in the air we breathe when we walk.

He is in the pure hands of the one who dedicates to correct the ills of the flesh.

God and His angels open the inner ear as to right combining and assimilation of foods. His angels will reveal the secrets in the grain, in the plant, in the fruit, in the herb.

God is in that one who intuits the spiritual alchemy within each healing herb.

God is in the pure and skilled physician who performs a service for the human body with total dedication. If he be a surgeon with an undisturbed mind, or a physician with love toward humanity, his ministering shall be of the Light. Such surgeons and physicians are channels for the Light.

The Guardian Angel and the Recording Angel stand nigh, ready to calm the emotions and to give clarity to the thoughts. If an emotionally disturbed person has the grace, the

Guardian Angel and the Recording Angel will unite; and the person, through self-research and self-discovery, will come to see the mercy of God. He will learn something of sympathy for others—and he will attain more of a forgiving heart.

The Mediative Healer knows that God is the Healer, and that he is but a channel. It is the work of the Mediative Healer to sustain his body of Light, that he may retain his equilibrium under all stress or strife. He knows that Jesus, the true Physician, will keep ajar and hold open the door to the healing helps of God.

11

ETHIC AND HEALING

During the birth of the world, God—the Eternal Spirit—did plant the greater seeds or the archetypes. These mighty atom-seeds or archetypes now shower upon men. All who have hearts of purity, all who have given of love, shall be taken into the net of the good Fisherman, the Lord Jesus—and the human spirit shall come forth. The human spirit shall work through those who serve in naive good. These now enter into an aroma of preciousness, expressing the true human spirit.

Every man is tried, that he may become a precious and anointed one. In victory he will stand with the Sovereign One, the Lord Jesus, who is the heart of the human spirit. He will see the Son of God, the Christ, as the mind of the human spirit.

When humanity has withstood its trial, the diamond of the soul shall come forth. Then shall the human spirit in mankind be perfected within the Christ Light. The human spirit shall set free the soul's light; and the Christ Light within the human spirit shall become a reality—and men shall know harmony.

Though all men struggle to rise, they shall reach the way of the human spirit. They will turn to the Christ who did bring the Way, and they will learn through the lips of Jesus what the Christ Spirit is saying. Where the Eternal Will of God is done, and where love is, the birth of the human spirit will become a reality.

Each person has an eternal ethic overdirecting his morality and his mercy. Each person has a soul-conscience overdirecting and supporting his self-esteem. To be dead to conscience is to become a vessel for evil works. To be born to conscience is to become a responsible son under the Will, Law, and Love of God.

Ethic is the science of rightness producing good. Constant ethic animated through healing works begins in mercy and ends in miracles.

To be healed, one should open his mind to receive instruction as to God's Equation. He should know that mercy is accompanied by the Angel of Hope who bestows vistas where there have been vacuums.

To learn that one cannot bend the Equation of God is the first disclosure of ethic at work. When the Will of God, the Law of God, and the ethic are at one, immortal manifestations begin. Living and eternal things are the result of these three working in unison.

Response to right formulas produces ethical actions or acts. When the Law of God is sealed into the hearts of pure men, the conscience exposes wrongdoing. Conscience works with the Recording Angels through dreams, events, situations.

Guilt is written on the foreheads of deviating men, and may be read by those having conscience. *Conscience united with ethic becomes prescience.* When men offend conscience on any level, they offend God. If a person seeks to influence another person to ignore his conscience, he is of antichrist.

To become a mediative spiritual healer, one must respond to his conscience and to all the tongues of conscience with which he has spoken throughout the aeons. The healer without conscience is a destroyer of body, health, emotions, mind. The priest or minister minus ethic and conscience is a Satanic agent perverting the Word of God. The initiate absent from conscience obscures his own light, and stands in the shadow of his soul.

The conscience may be rectified by repentance, pure motive, and pure actions. Good works without thought of reward or gain result in grace. When conscience is united with the Will of God, the Word of God falls into the mind— instructing, healing.

God gives life and light to him who responds to Law. Response to Law directs and gives purpose to talents, gifts, missions, covenants. To come under the Law is to be purged, chastened, cleansed. To observe and live under the Law will give sacred-rightness or ethic to one's motive and intent.

God is not a God of revenge. He is a God of love. His Law IS. His Love corrects, shapes, supports. Abuse of Law attracts correction. He who observes Law comes under quick correction; he who consents to God's Love through Law, receives instantaneous reproving. When God's Law is known, and yet offended through irresponsible acts, the consequence is suffering and soul chastening.

Crisis in life is a compulsive overthrow of deviation. Emergency in health or accident holds the key to the resources of the soul.

Man reads small portions of his soul's record in sickness, dreams, and death. His moral health, his ethic, his good obedience to the Law of God are recorded in Heaven.

There will never be enough tongues to tell or give record of the manifold diseases of man, for diseases come without number when Equation is denied.

Each man interprets his suffering and the blessing of his healing through the eyes of his evolvement. Each man must give his testimony,

and his spirit will tell him what to say in his
testimony. There is a testimony of the spirit—
and there is a tongue of the soul disclosing the
true cause in sickness.

To be used as a healer for God, one should
make passive his pressures; he should make
quiet his assertiveness. He should make his faith
well through God's Will, for doubt divides the
mind and repels the Succoring and Ministering Angels.

Angels cannot stand in proximity to doubt.
Doubt is of the dark. Faith is of the light. When
faith is whole and complete, one invites the
angels' help. The angels come nigh to the peaceful heart, giving healing peace to him who calls.

A contrite heart is never far from God's perfect Equation. The Succoring Angels sustain a
contrite heart and mind. The Succoring Angels
send their thoughts to the contrite—teaching of
mercy united to timing. Upon the step of mercy
begins the upward walk of restitution and the
resulting benefits of renunciation.

Sickness is rectification. For every ailment in
human form there is intercession. The angels
make haste to respond to the cries of men. The
angels assure men that God knows and hears
their prayer, their call.

Sickness is a soul discipline. All disciplines
are to teach self-control and to produce spiritual
usefulness.

Sickness is initiatory. Some sicknesses produce elimination; some are for cleansing; some are for quickening. All offer new birth to the will, emotions, and thoughts.

Grace-therapies, stemming from a reverent and faithful heart, heal. Grace-therapy is a divine therapy—an anastasis of holiness, an apostolic grace. The reaches of the soul are illimitable. Where need is, the Father doeth the works without end.

To those who would hear, the Spirit cautions and says, "Let him who would hold up prayers for the fevered, the sick, the weak, the lame, the halt, and the blind first exorcise the negations or demons in his own heart and mind."

To become a healer for God one must first enter into the desert of cleansing, as did the Lord. Until then, he must lean upon the angels to armor and support him; he must call on the intercession of the Saints and the Presences of Heaven to give impetus to his prayers.

The healer should make a covenant to purity; he should accept the initiations qualifying him to become a healer for God. He should keep the castle of his spirit inviolate with a loving heart, a charitable mind. Through experience he will gather an internship of ethics, that he may become forever a channel of ministering, healing good.

Preservation of life is stewardship for God.

All spiritual healers should work with and lean upon the restoring power of Eternal Spirit.

The eternal tenderness of God is waiting to give merciful blessings through love. The love of the healer is a singular life-artery of restoration. When united with ethic and the Equation of God, health becomes holy and complete.

Love is a supernal fiat supporting the science of rightness or ethic. Love is the kernel or life breath of ethic. Living works are insupportable without ethic; without love, ethic is dead.

Spiritual amnesia or forgetfulness of God is caused by repetitive accentuation upon things negative. To see only the faulty, the false; to ignore the basic restorer of life (God's love); to continually think materialistic thoughts— these famish the Divine interflow between man and God.

To have access to spiritual health, one must love life as he loves God, for God is life. He must unite himself with life and become one who lives for God.

The will to live comes from God. When one unites his love of life with the will to live, he will receive the restoring grace. The spiritual power of manifestation will overcome disease, fevers, infirmities, infections.

God has given life. He has also given certain preservative, restorative balances to maintain life. The life of the soul is the center of health.

When one prays for the healing of another person, he crosses the threshold of the soul of the one for whom he is praying.

God gave the life. God will preserve and restore the life. When one turns to God for health, he will be healed as God wills, not as the one praying wills.

Any degree of personal will-healing invokes an exchange of magnetism. The one using his will to heal another takes upon himself something of the soul-debts of the one sick. The one submitting to a magnetic will-healer surrenders his will to the one seeking to heal him.

Healings fostered by human magnetism are an expression of Simon-the-Magician powers, rather than the methods of the Son of Man, whose miracles of healing exceeded the suggestive and persuasive marvels of mental magic.

Persons who pray that *their* will be done, rather than the Father's Will, offend the ethic of healing. Prayers colored by man's will and unclarified desiring intrude upon the initiation concealed in sickness.

All initiations are accompanied, to some degree, by mortification or humiliation. As one approaches lesser self-genesis, mortification and humility trials are more frequently experienced, for one must dissolve the egotistical shell formed from many self-willed and vain actions.

When mortification is experienced through

sickness, this is an agreement between the soul and the body. When mortification is experienced through loss of possessions, one has made an agreement to travel light, that he may spread the Light.

To plough up new soil—that is, to acquire new habits of health—requires will. To make acrid soil sweet requires purging. Health of the soul provides a sweet soil ready for the seed, producing a good harvest in right season.

Neglect of the physical body results in ill health. Sickness inevitably occurs when accumulative interior ills of the emotional, etheric, and mental bodies converge. To be ill in all four bodies is to invite the Death Angel. (All forms of sickness are little deaths.)

The cause producing sickness is first imprinted upon the lesser etheric body. All defections from natural law protecting one's physical body produce etheric infection. Such sicknesses appear first as emotional irritation and mental discontent.

Spiritual restoring balm is centered in the higher etheric body. Nature's restoring balm is centered in the lesser etheric body. The restoring power of the lesser etheric body is received from the elements, the atmosphere, the rays of the sun, and from vital foods. The higher etheric body revitalizes the lesser etheric body during prayer, meditation, mantramic speaking, and during sleep. The restoring power of the higher etheric body is received from the Higher Self, which knows not sickness nor ill health. The Higher Self is at one with the image of the Father and with the greater Host or Hierarchs who watch over the forming, molding, and shaping of men.

To stay constant to the Will of God provides one with spiritual vitality or anastasis grace. Through anastasis grace, one may restore his own body, and he may also restore the bodies of others.

The higher etheric body, a perfected body, does not record sickness or experience it. When one turns his will, emotions, and thoughts in the direction of spiritual health, the higher degrees of light within the higher etheric body will still the electric dissensions in the lesser etheric body.

When one is negative in emotions and thoughts, using the lower degrees of light in emotion and thought, the currents within the lesser etheric body move in a contraclockwise manner; the nervous system is disorganized. The result is pain, confusion, decay, degeneration.

The will and the nerves are twin systems through which the soul may raise man to a higher degree of consciousness. To dwell for long periods upon negative conditions or situations devitalizes the will, and the nerves become irritating communicators. A forceful will over-energizes the vitality of the lesser etheric body; the etheric sheathes protecting the nervous system are stripped, and one's better emotions are immobilized.

The human blood is a powerful mirror through which the human spirit pictures the images of man's perfect origin or eternal ancestry.

When men were formed in the Edenic state, certain atoms of the higher etheric body produced the beginning of the cell system. All cells contain bacterial life. When bacteria are balanced, the alternates produce health rather than sickness.

The bacteria in the cell system, tissues, organs, muscles, arteries, glands and blood are necessary agents serving the ego and the soul. Bacteria accomplish a work of health when faith is centered in God as the One Life, the One Will directing the creation of man.

The alternate action sustaining all things in this cosmic eternity works also in the human body. Sickness is experienced in the physical body when the alternates set the organs at variance with one another. The division of the cells in the body is also the work of the greater alternates. Should one reach a state of self-inharmony, in which the emotions and thoughts are antagonistic to one another, the cells move out of their timing in the alternates; they fail to slough off the dying cells. The blood stream generates infection, and the nervous system records the inharmony as pain.

There are twelve stigmata or pain antennas in the lesser etheric body. These stigmata are sensitive points gained through pain endured in sacrificial acts in former or previous lives. Each spiritual initiate has some degree of stigmata sensitivity. The stigmata enable the spiritual initiate to remain in sympathy with the need of the world. Were it not for the stigmata sensitivity, the initiate would be opaque and blind to the suffering in the world; and he would become calloused and subjected to materialistic compromise. The stigmata are also the means through which he drains off his own mental and emotional poisons.

The spiritual healing initiate, or Mediative Healer, is more sensitive than other persons because of his awakened stigmata. When one is depleted in his healing work, he has in some manner offended the use of the stigmata. The initiate at all times should seek to translate the suffering of others into Light, and thus fulfill a selfless healing work. To linger overlong upon the thought of the grief or the pain presented to him will irritate the stigmata, and the initiate will find himself diverted from his path of effort.

The stigmata cannot function for anyone who has spiritual pride. Through the stigmata, the initiate is always in harmony with humbleness, giving, serving, reverence, charitableness, and the preserving of good. The stigmata keep him continually aware of the sacrificial grace of the soul; therefore he thinks less of himself and more of others.

Pray for the sick, and God will heal them.

Pray for the Will of God to manifest health in right timing.

Prepare your prayers with ethic in heart and mind.

Teach the one under your prayers to free the mind from regret. Teach him the difference between regret and repentance. Tell him that regret is a devitalizer, while repentance vitalizes and shows a better way.

12

MEDIATIVE HEALING

Men need help. Men need the help of the angels. Men need the works of the Healing Ministry. From every source in Heaven there are assets of healing. And there are many sources of mediative healing helps in the physical world. Any of these may cool the fevers of the mind and still the frenzies of the emotions.

The majority of sicknesses are the result of a burdened soul or self-reproach in some form. When Jesus was in the physical world, He healed certain ailments by saying, "Thy sins are forgiven thee. Go and sin no more." Jesus recognized that man's guilt produced deformities and sicknesses, unhappiness and sorrow.

And as Jesus passed by, he saw a man which was blind from his birth. And his disciples asked him, saying, Master, who did sin, this man, or his parents, that he was born blind.
—St. John 9:1,2

The disciples asked Jesus to define whether the man's blindness was caused by previous-life guilt, or whether it was caused by the guilt of his parents. A child may enter the world with

soul-debts to rectify, or he may enter a family-
atom heavily laden with guilt, and thus take
upon himself something of the conscience of the
family-atom.

Jesus answered, Neither hath this man sinned, nor his parents:
but that the works of God should be made manifest in him.
—St. John 9:3

In healing the blind man, Jesus revealed that
the man's conscience was uncolored by guilt,
and that the family into which he had been born
was uncolored by guilt.

In some instances sickness is experienced by
a catalyst soul who enters the world to be an
atonement offering for the guilt of the world.
The blind man had taken upon himself something of the guilt or conscience of the world,
rather than having sinned himself in former
lives.

There are some sicknesses in the world which
are suffered by worthy persons, that a very
special work of God may be done—thereby
cleansing the world conscience. When the soul's
record is unshadowed by guilt, one discerns a
definite plan whereby God's work may be fulfilled. Healings of such sicknesses help the
world conscience to maintain its equilibrium.

In ripe timing, the blind man was healed by
Jesus—confirming not only Jesus' miraculous
gifts, but also that when a soul is ready, his
affliction is lifted from him.

To die to the errors imprinted upon the soul's medallion, one must undergo, over a period of many lives, the fiery trials consuming the errors of the past. However, all pain is purifying fire. To know pain is also to know light. When light is greater than fire, pain ceases and health begins.

The spine, the instrument for the will, correlates to "Aaron's rod." One who lives within the Will of God learns of the disciplining power of Aaron's rod—and he becomes a channel for the Will of God. A lethargic, wilful, or disobedient will produces degeneration of the health-giving vitalities of the physical body.

Suffering offers two things: proving and reproving. Each sickness contains a way in which man may prove the Will of God for him, and offers to him a way in which he may become obedient to the reproving from God. When one accepts God's reproving, the light of the Jesus Ethic is within him. Through faith in the just Law of God, one proves the perfect manifestation within healing; and he also accepts the fact that he is being reproved through sickness and suffering. "He that hateth reproof shall die." (Proverbs 15:10)

When one opens his mind to *what* is being said through sickness, he will receive the blessing of healing manifestation. If one consents not to the reproving within sickness, he will experience continued de-manifestation, and will fail to respond to healing. If he wishes not to live, or has a secret desire to flee from life, de-manifestation will continue within his body. Such persons fail to respond to the healing power within the spirit of manifestation.

There are seven levels of suffering or pain:

1. The suffering one undergoes to obtain purity or chastity. This suffering, in its lowest aspect, is manifested due to one's failure to channel, purely, the sexual nature.

2. The suffering one undergoes due to having unwisely used a presumptuous and dominating will. When one has abused his will, he invites dominance from others. He suffers frustration and repression through outer conditions and persons. This causes irritability, devitalization, and spiritual anemia; the cells, the nerves, the muscles, the glands, and the organs of the body are slower to respond to the animating power of his soul.

3. The suffering caused by lack of co-ordination with the laws of Nature, and lack of obedience to the laws of God. This suffering comes from the will to hoard, retain, or possess, and causes the slowing down of the senses—thereby short-circuiting the soul faculties.

4. All suffering related to the desires, feelings, and emotions is due to an unresponsiveness to love, irreverence in the use of love, and a denial of the existence of God's love for man.

5. The healing power of the word is a gift from God, and may become the most godly power one possesses. The healing power of the word relates to the ethic concealed in the words of the Lord Jesus. Anguish, futility, and suffering are caused by the abuse of the spoken word. Untruths, cursing, or the use of profane oaths despoil the sacred logos given to man. To slander another invites vilification of one's self. Loose and careless conversation is an invitation to shallow companions with thoughtless minds.

6. The neglect of one's intellectual and mental resource and reserve, as given of God, will produce an atrophying of thought, resulting in mental suffering or anxiety. When one entertains thoughts of avarice, lust, malice, covetousness, doubt, and greed, or when he delights in critical thinking, he darkens the light of his mind, and shuts away the Christ Mind in himself. One of the greatest errors, which leads man into suffering, is his lack of cultivation of the mind.

7. The greatest suffering, impossible to describe to one of a materialistic nature, is the suffering experienced by the seeker of God who is temporarily separated from God. This suffering is called *spiritual dryness,* and is due to some initiatory trial in which one has failed to see the Spirit of God at work within all things, persons, actions, conditions, events.

The Mediative Healer will see many degrees of suffering. He should pray that he condemn not any person. At all times, he should avoid any conclusive analysis as to the cause of suffering; he should remember that mediative works carry with them an anointing balm, which will give ease to whatever degree of suffering is made manifest.

Each healing contains something of Heaven. Man without Heaven is a darkened island unto himself. Response to Light is innate, natural. The body, the cells, the blood, and the bones of man have been envisioned in Heaven; therefore, it is natural in the order of creation that the organs, the emotions, and thoughts of man respond to Light. The consistency of all organisms being of Light, it is in accord with God's Equation that all men respond, in some manner, to Light.

When one consecrates himself to heal, he becomes an ambassador for Heaven. He expands his body of Light, and he comes to know more and more of Mediative Ignition.

The Mediative Healer is an igniter—that is, he ignites the Light in the person for whom he prays, and he extends the range of his own Mediative Ignition. In time, the Mediative Healer increases his degree of Light; and his healing works become a tangible testimony of Heaven.

In the lesser self-genesis age, the most prevalent sickness is that of mental depression and mental imbalance. One cause of mental suffering is the shadowing of the egotistical shell against the soul's light. The egotistical shell has been built from self-centered acts in this life and in many past lives.

Mental depression may be caused by either pride or inflexibility. Pride makes rigid the mental atoms, and prevents spontaneity in thought. The inflexible mind suffocates the mental body and the thought process, and shuts away the renewing, the revitalizing and inspiring thoughts sent forth from the soul.

Another cause of mental depression is agnosticism plus skeptical thinking or thoughts. Agnosticism is the result of misdirected beliefs and dead-end instruction in this life or in previous lives.

Mental depression is sometimes caused by subjection to devitalizing entities from the lower astral regions. This is the result of the desire to subject oneself to the subtle worlds, so that psychical powers may be used for gain.

Depression, wilfully sustained in thought, is a selfish indulgence, leading one to sin, to err. A person who persistently dwells upon negation invites antagonistic resistances in the body; he becomes his own contagion and manifests what he continually dwells upon. To be constantly aware of what is wrong is to invoke the judgment side of law, and thus nullify the mercy and love of God.

THE EMOTIONAL BODY AND MEDIATIVE HEALING

The emotional body, ovoid in shape, is being continually pummelled and sculptured by one's thoughts, feelings, and actions. However, the true forming of the emotional body is accomplished through love. When the Mediative Healer has a total and complete love for God, and is free of the claims in self-love, he becomes a channel through which the love of God may enter the emotional body of a person in need.

Love is the anointer, and life is the restorer. When these are united with the power of Spirit, the one needing help will respond to the love-healing helps. Let each healer emanate love. And let him also transmit to the one in need the sense of worthiness; for the emotional body is the body expressing a feeling of unworthiness. Therefore, the first thought in the Mediative

Healer's mind is that the person in need, being of God, is worthy of the love of God; and he prays that he may be a loving , selfless, healing channel for the helps from God.

Jesus saw men in the forming stage. He loved them in spite of their frailties, for He saw God in each man. Jesus also knew that a deep sense of guilt dwelt in the feelings of man. When He healed, He knew that if the healing were to be permanent, man must erase all feelings of guilt, and also determine to repent and enter into a new way of life. Thus, Jesus said to some, "Go and sin no more."

The emotional body is the body of response. It is most directly connected with the soul's pulsation, in that it has the power of receiving and the power of repelling—that is, it works with expansion and contraction. When one thinks of his emotional body as being in a continued state of inhaling and exhaling, of receiving and discarding, his emotional body thus becomes more real to him; and he is better able to unite himself with the expansion and contraction power of the soul's pulsation.

Before Mediative Healing helps may manifest for the one in need, there must be a willing response, not only from the thoughts of the one in need, but also from his emotional body. Failure to respond to Healing Mediation is caused by the incapacity to respond to love.

When there is fear of love, or if there is any form of revulsion towards love, the healing helps are thwarted.

Emotional suffering comes to persons who have cynically used love as lust over many lives. The feeling of being unworthy for love is produced from past-life sins against the love of man and mankind. The sensual person suffers emotionally because he relies upon his sense-experience rather than the deep and reverent aspect of his feelings.

When one has been bruised through love association in past lives, he has a timidity, and refuses to yield up his love in this life. He distrusts the intuition of his feelings. He is fearful of giving freely of himself and of his love to anyone—for he is fearful of being wounded once more.

When one dedicates to become a healing channel for God, he should seek to clarify and define his correlating to the Great Physician, the Lord Jesus. Those who correlate to the knees of Jesus have the power to make of their prayers healing arteries for mankind. Those who correlate to His hands have the healing power of the laying on of the hands.

The true laying on of the hands is not through any form of mesmeric or magnetic passes, but is manifested through the higher etheric body; for the higher etheric body is chaste and devoid of sullied and unclean magnetism. The Mediative Healer uses the technique of the laying on of the hands in the Night Ministry rather than through daytime works. However, if the Mediative Healer has perfected a sustained alignment with his higher etheric body, he can, while in the physical body, use the etheric power of healing through the laying on of the hands. This occurs only in the rare instance of an extreme act of grace. This healing cannot be compared with the magnetic and mesmeric laying on of the hands and the exchange of magnetism from one body to another.

If one is filled with the feeling of self-sufficiency as to his own healing power, he is merely a conductor of magnetism, which moves against the electrical imbalance in the body he seeks to heal. His ministrations are saturated with personal magnetism. Therefore, one should not place himself in the hands of any person who has conceit or self-love.

Spiritual healing consummated through the higher etheric body neutralizes the magnetic and electrical powers in the physical body of the healer and in the body of the one to be healed. Thus, there is no transmitting of soiled energies. Where there is an act of grace, and the power of the laying on of the hands is called forth spiritually, a healing may be produced where there has been an injury to the physical body, or a healing may manifest to alleviate some weakness of the physical body. In chronic conditions, a reversal of currents may be produced within the lesser etheric body. The pure laying on of the hands may also awaken the dynamic power of feeling within the emotional body, overcoming the oppressions of fear within the feelings.

And he laid his hands on her: and immediately she was made straight, and glorified God.

—St. Luke 13:13

THE INWARD SELF AND THE PHYSICAL BODY

The ethical Mediative Healer does not think of himself as the diagnostician or the healer. He knows that God is the Healer, and that the law of God is the diagnostician. When sickness occurs, he is aware that some law has been offended. Pain in the physical body is the compass needle pointing toward the theme of deviation and imbalance.

In time, the Mediative Healer will come to see and recognize something of the inner causes underlying the outer manifestation of an unsound body.

When man offends the laws of the physical body, there is war in the members of the body; the organs contend with one another; the higher and lower emotions compete with one another; and the thoughts enter into conflict, dissensions, pain, and anguish. The living functions of the body become disorganized. From this comes a sick body. To bring health to the body, and peace to the emotions and thoughts, one must resolve to return to the laws of God.

When the body is disobedient to the laws of God, the result is imperfection, making one a vessel in part—and the soul has an uneasy resting place. The Mediative Healer should teach those he would help to acknowledge and accept the just laws of God, and to follow and obey the laws of God. The Mediative Healer should provide himself with all channels and resources of prayer, believing in the grace of God, the works of God, and the Will of God.

To prepare the physical body as a better vessel for Divine Spirit, every building block must be in place—each block giving off the emanation of pure Spirit. One should pray that the physical body become a choice vessel for Divine Spirit.

Disappointment comes from faulty expectations. Dissatisfaction comes from denying the creative aspect in the soul. Discontentment comes from failing to build an orderly atmosphere necessary for the life of the physical body.

Disorder is an invitation to disaster. One offends God's law of order when the physical environment is disordered or disorganized. The Mediative Healer should inspire the one he would help to bring order to his habits, to organize his environment, and to live within the rhythmic pattern of life, so that he may have a lasting and permanent benefit from prayer and spiritual healing helps.

Outwardly, the physical body may appear to be corruptible and in a continuing state of transition, flux, and change. Through the work of mediative healing, the physical body can become transformed into a radiant and worthy vessel for God. When the physical body is communicable to the inward self, the physical body becomes an intricate and supersensitive instrument responding to the inherent soul and to the indestructible spirit.

In time, the Mediative Healer will discern that when one fails to communicate with the inward self, the physical body is inclined to respond to the negations of the world. When one is wholly materialistic, the tone of the organs, nerves, cells, and the tempo of the emotions and thoughts are expressed with gross insensitivity. The result is a fearful person at war with the competitive spirit in the world.

The Mediative Healer should remember that, regardless of how materialistic a person has become, if the person is directed to his inward self, a manifestation through grace will occur.

When one devotes his life to material gain, he misconstrues the meaning of life. When grace enters the life of the materialistic person, he is made aware that he is insufficient unto himself; this is the grace of his soul preparing him for deeper sensitivity and for acknowledgment of the inward self.

When a materialistic person responds to mediative healing, he will undergo one or more transitions in his attitudes toward the use of his physical body:

He will seek to become more selective as to the habits of his body.

His body will refuse to assimilate and digest certain foods.

He will feel himself helpless to cope with the weakness apparent in his physical body. He will become more dependent on efficient and ethical help from others.

He will begin to recognize certain laws governing the body, objects, and possessions.

He will learn that his happiness depends not upon himself, but upon the approbation and love of others near and by.

The physical body is a transitory vehicle of convenience subject to momentary and daily death. When one has earned a good physical body through perfect physical works in a former life, he is aware of the restoring life within his physical body overdirected by the Eternal Spirit. Thus, he is devoid of egotism as related to physical competence and capability.

When a person is highly evolved, he is less likely to duplicate ancestral weaknesses in his physical body. When a person has lived in sentient-atom experience in former lives, he is more likely to inherit the physical weaknesses of his ancestral stream. Mediative healing may enable a person to rise above ancestral inclinations and tendencies. The Mediative Healer should seek to reveal the true ancestry to such persons—that is, all men are created in the likeness of "our Father which art in Heaven." Thus, our Father is the true Parent or Ancestor.

The self-genesis age now approaching men will produce many ailments hitherto unknown to man, and will also introduce into the lives of all persons certain habit formulas for living as yet unkown in the world.

When men have attained the higher level of self-genesis, there shall be introduced into the world a perfect rhythm of daily living. This will include five working hours, five recreational hours, five creative hours. From this, man will achieve the highest ethic as to life and its purpose. Needless to say, this perfect rhythm for the physical life is impossible for the average person in the present society. However, all persons, who would utilize their physical lives to the uttermost, should pray to attain a perfect rhythm expressing the creative life.

Every deviation from the laws governing the four bodies must be set aright. Until one agrees to be healed, and resigns himself to the life-restoring love of the Father, he cannot receive healing.

There is a third element existing in all human organisms. Until science and medicine discover this element, they will continue to grapple with the alternating virilities in the human organism—the destroying virility and the building virility.

The third element in healing is a restoring vitality or *third vitality* under the command of soul and spirit. When physicians, therapeutic laymen, or metaphysical healers are assisted by this third vitality, there is a manifestation of absolute healing.

All persons with spiritual hearts and minds acknowledge that health responds to selfless prayer and that miracles are worked through undeviating faith.

The higher mind is a golden germinal vortex of receptivity to the archetypes of the Eternal Spirit. The higher mind is a non-judging and non-condemning mind. A critical mind is an instrument for negation. A mind filled with true acceptance of God's Equation results in an anointing mercy and healing.

Before one receives a healing, his soul is searched by his Recording Angel; his debts are

weighed; his motives, his faith, and his purpose
are balanced one against the other. During this
period, the overzealous or intense person enters
into a state of mental fire; the lethargic person
enters into a cold state of melancholy and de-
spair. If a high fever is manifested, the person
opens deep recesses of conscience. If there be
no fever, deep depression will enter into the
mind. This may be likened to the after-death
purgatory.

There are degrees of Heaven inherent in
man. If he has within himself good, he is responsive to the plateau of Heaven where dwell
the Cherubim Angels; this plateau will enable
him to achieve integrity, honor, charity. If he
has within himself both peace and good, he will
be responsive to the plateau of Heaven where
dwell the Saints; this is the plateau of equanimity and serenity. If he has the grace to have
obtained a portion of wisdom, he will respond
to another plateau of Heaven—the plateau of
instruction—where dwell the Seraphim and the
Great Immortals. As he increases in his wisdom,
and obeys the instruction of Heaven, he shall
be given greater understanding of the Kingdom
of God.

CONTEMPLATIVE HEALING THOUGHTS

I

Now bring thy house—thy physical body—into holiness.
Now bring thy house into green pastures—that is, give
    nutriment to thy body.
Now bring thy body into peace environments, and give
    nourishment to the esthetic responses in the body.
Now bring thy body into cultures,
        that thou mayest feed the mind,
        that thou mayest not be desolate,
        or lose sight of what God hath created
        through the souls of men.
Live thou in that which is the peace of exchange in
    relationships.
And pray that thou shalt be placed in thy homeplace
        with those who make of thee a holy partner in Spirit.
For this is thy house, thy home, thy building of God.
When these things are manifest, thou mayest be said to have
    a temple of God.

When thy virtues come out of thy chaste self, thou shalt
    lack not discrimination.
When thy works come out of thy creative self, thou shalt
    lack not for companions of Spirit and soul who remind
    thee of God and creation.
When the musics of Heaven sound and expand thy soul,
    thou shalt touch all levels of creation, of art, of music.
And thou shalt find a linguistic tongue to speak to man,
    for he who is a creator hath a universal voice.
He is a cosmic initiate who speaks through the arts and
    who speaks in manners by which men are lifted and
    ennobled.

II

Let each one remember that he is not just an organism. Let
him remember that he is not a lump of materiality or
a deposit in inert matter. Let him know that he is life
quickened—and that, even as life is quickened and has
its potential, so doth it increase itself with quickening,
and so may it restore itself.

Let peace of mind bring regeneration to the physical body.
Let love within the heart's flame bring healing to the physical body and to the emotions.
And let this bring the warming love which men need to be
secure in their inward selves.
When men have lost communion with their inward selves,
the world produces inferior persons.

III

In the night hours, thou didst touch the streams of peace.
In the night hours, thou didst touch the way in which thy
heart did come to ease itself; and thy wounds, thy
scars, did rest themselves in the oil of the Healing
Cloisters of Heaven.
For that which purifieth the bodies of men through fra-
grances and that which anointeth men is also that which
cometh from the Healing Cloisters of Heaven.

Be thou not bruised through temperament, but let temperament be under thy command, and learn that thy temperament is as the sound of the music which cometh
from the player's hand—that is, which thy will doth
direct.

If thy will hath developed a temperament, learn that thy will can develop a greater and more noble quality, beyond temperament, which is called that Self which endears itself rather than that self which would display itself.

For temperament is that display which men see; but that which is noble is that which men know and experience.

In Christ thou art loved. In Christ stand in peace. In Christ fulfill the way in which the Word hath healed the wounds; and the oil of peace shall overcome the ills of the temperament.

The ills of the temperament are first of pride, of vanity.

The ills of the temperament come from foolish expectations.

The ills of the temperament are displayed in selfishness, in impatience, in irritations, in dissatisfaction.

Let the ills of the temperament come to rest in the oil of the Healing Cloisters of Heaven, in that oil which is charged with the fire of Spirit, in that oil which hath not of itself any thing which burns or stings, but only an emollient of peace, of healing.

Peace unto thee in Christ.

Peace.

13

HEALING TECHNIQUE AND MANTRAMS

The mighty Will of God
is willing my life.
The mighty Will of God
is setting me free.
The mighty Will of God
is speaking into my will.

My mentality is an instrument
for the mighty Will of God.
When I live in the mighty Will of God,
I know His supreme Will
is the One Will.

If I be ill,
the mighty Will of God heals me.
If I am confused,
the mighty Will of God is my therapy.
I give praise
for the mighty Will of God.

The Will of God
has sounded creation.
And the Will of God
is mighty,
eternal.

The desire to heal comes from one's spiritual reservoir or medallion of grace. A heart rhythm is set up in a healer-to-be. This works as a mighty compassion and mercy toward mankind. Even as Jesus wept, so does the healer-to-be grieve when he beholds the burdens of men. His grieving continues until he opens his medallion of grace, and receives the helps of the angels and the Holy Presences of Heaven. Through prayer he organizes his spiritual faculties, and develops a compact, illuminative body of healing action. When he meditates, contemplates, prays, and speaks mantramic logos words of healing love, he is given a sacred and holy insight into the needs of men; he becomes an instrument of healing love and light. Through the angelic mediation, he may approach without intrusion the soul-debts of men on any level or in any degree.

When the Mediative Healer has built a body of light and love, he enters into an experience with his higher faculties unlike any other occurring to man on earth. He quickens his pace in evolvement. He begins to overcome heavy soul-debts of his present life and of former lives, that he may qualify to receive an unending spiritual sustenance from the Eternals.

Mediative Healers need no announcement in the world. They *are*. Their soul-grace divinely appoints them to their environment where men

in need shall seek them out. The tumults
and unrest in men's emotions and egotistical
thoughts, moving painfully against their souls'
desire for peace, will direct them to one who
holds the sacred key to their release from pain
and suffering. Mediative healing will enable
them to overcome feelings of unworthiness; they
will cleanse the flaws and faults revealed in
their thought worlds. And their souls will instruct them as to the reality of Heaven. Mediative Healers are grace for the world, and are
sent in timing to the need of the world.

Great healers of nations are pure statesmen
in alignment with the Guardian Angels of a
nation. Great patriarchal leaders of races bring
a cleansing moral law to the races, so that race
grace may be sustained. Great healers of tribal-
genesis and family-genesis are to be found in
science and medicine; such healers also bring
many material helps to make lighter the burdens in the world. Truly dedicated scientists,
psychiatrists, medical physicians, and metaphysicians work with the greater Guardian
Angels in direct alignment with Jesus.

The spiritually dedicated healers who carry
the light as Healing Mediators in the world
work with mediative light as part of the great
spectrum of the Christ. They are trained through
countless lives to be selfless healers. They are
aligned with all degrees of suffering and pain

in the world and with the world degree of grace. Thus, they may manifest their works of grace, and be insulated from the fiery degrees of initiation experienced by those whom they would heal. Such great healers come to work with co-atom Mediative Healers in the visible and invisible worlds. They make up a sacred conclave. They see man as he is, rather than as he thinks he is. They see him as he is to be, rather than as he has been.

Mediative Healers now enter the earth stream and work both in imparting spiritual wisdom and in fulfilling a Healing Ministry. God works through them to heal the impossible and the improbable in right timing. Their hearts are in perfect alignment with the heartbeat of the world, or the great pulse of God which determines the well-being of man.

Mediative Healers who are young in their experience leave no stone unturned in their seeking the right techniques of healing. These healers know sacredly within themselves the reverent approach to healing helps and turn always their eyes to the Lord of Healing, the Jesus One. They seek to perfect themselves that they may become "like Him." They are open to instruction. They are pliable and teachable. They are unprejudiced, and begin their alignment in mediation by becoming as pure springs of clear water. They are uncritical and non-judging. With minds cleansed and emotions free from any glamour or glitter of the temporary or the false, they are enabled to sustain selfless thought in equal degree with selfless love, in which faith may work with will in moral and spiritual strength. They are loving—and willing to serve. They are dedicated, ethical channels for healing light and love.

And he sent them to preach the kingdom of God, and to heal the sick.

—St. Luke 9:2

There are five strong healing impulses received from the Spiritual Worlds each day: on arising; mid-morning (10 a.m.); 12 noon; dusk; and 11 p.m. The five mediative healing tides correspond to the five senses and to the five soul-faculties of man. Any one of these tides may be used by the Mediative Healer if he would benefit by the incoming power of regeneration sent mediatively from the Spiritual Worlds.

The Mediative Healing Technique should be used only once a day. Dusk mediative healing is more effective for those who rely upon the mediative healing love of the Lord Jesus.

The Mediative Healer should continue the Mediative Healing Technique until he is assured that healing grace is being manifested.

MEDIATIVE HEALING TECHNIQUE

1. Mediative healing begins by prayer on the knees.

2. After prayer, one should be seated. He should prepare to become a mediative channel for healing by speaking a *before-meditation mantram.*

3. Gently close the eyes. Hold love in the heart (ten seconds).

4. Visualize Light stilling the thoughts on the level of the brow (ten seconds).

5. Raise the Light to the crown of the head; hold the Light steadily, and then visualize the person or persons to be healed. Each person should be held in the Light singly. (This portion of the Mediative Healing Technique should not extend longer than five minutes.)

6. While holding each person in the Light, speak an *Angel to Angel Mantram.*

7. Conclude by speaking an *after-meditation mantram.*

8. Optional: prayer on the knees. With complete conviction and faith, give thanks to the Father.

BEFORE-MEDITATION MANTRAMS

I am more than a portion of debris
cast upon a careless wave.
I am life seeking the creative Word.
Life cannot die.
Light cannot die.
Let the immortal light
and the resurrected power of the Lord Jesus
speak their perfect word
into my heart, my mind, my soul.

*

The music of Heaven
builds a geometry,
making a diadem or crown
for my thoughts.
May my crown of thoughts
remain in the Christ-Light—
and, therefore, overcome the crown of thorns
pressing heavily upon the thinking of men in
     the world.

*

When God's time has come for me,
I shall remember the key to the door
of the quiet place.
And each day
I shall enter the door of the quiet place
and commune with the true self.

*

In peace and in the light,
my works of day and night
come under the protection
of the angels,
who know my way
and guide me.

*

My spiritual garment,
woven with the threads of golden wisdom,
is a fabric of love united—silken, golden.
My spiritual garment
is a seamless garment.
I pray that I shall wear it with honor,
with love,
and with dignity.

*

May the Lord strengthen me
and clarify my purpose.
And may the Light
increase my stature,
for I would walk
in mediation with godly men.
And I would give tongue
to the Word of God.

*

Wherever I walk,
light shall be.
Light shall resolve
and heal the wounds

near and by.
Millions of miracles will come,
if I surrender my will
to the Will of God.

*

How glorious is the pearl of my inner being
purchased by the trials of many days.
I shall guard and cherish it.
I shall give praise
for my luminous pearl.

*

Lord, let me come under Thy divinity;
and let my soul know Thy height and depth,
Thy length and breadth.
And let the light of my soul
become a perpetual light
upon Thy altar place—
a light going not out—
speaking my sacred name,
sounding my eternal tone.

*

Wherever there is light and love
there is the music of Heaven,
a symphony of God.
Let me listen to the symphony of God,
swelling,
sounding.
And let me know the grandeur
of God's Universe.

*

May the peace of my devotion
be as a winged dove.
And may my thoughts and heart
be kindled with light.

*

I am a soul in a body.
I am immortal.
The glorious light within my soul,
speaking into my mind and heart,
awaits my knowing.
If there be anything between me and the light,
I pray that it be removed,
that I may know the Eternal in everything.
The Law of God is order.
The Law of God is creation.
The Law of God is euphony, beauty.
The law of my timing is in my hands.
If I will,
I may come into timing with my soul;
and I will know.

ANGEL TO ANGEL MANTRAMS

Beloved, my angel speaks unto thy angel.
If it is the Will of the Father,
may you be healed
in the name of the Christ.

*

Beloved, my angel speaks unto thy angel.
May thy tears
become as holy dew,
and bring unto thee a true blessing.
Open thy heart to the joy of tomorrow,
and receive the tidings of good
prepared for thee.

*

Beloved, my angel speaks unto thy angel.
How glorious to see thy freedom,
thy inner light,
thy joy, thy countenance.
I give thanks
for the soul light within thee.
I give thanks for thy peace.

*

Beloved, my angel speaks unto thy angel.
May the tide of thy soul
go out,
and may it return.
And may thy soul instruct thee,
and give thee comfort and peace,
and joy in the acceptance of the real for thee.

*

Beloved, my angel speaks unto thy angel.
Let thy hope
and thy love
and thy peace
become as a sweet fragrance,
and remind thee

of the joyful time and day
and the renewal of the good way
in Christ.

*

Beloved, my angel speaks unto thy angel.
Know thou art loved.
May the tenderness of God's Love
warm and heal thee,
and give thee peace.
May the anxiety within thy thoughts
look to the Light and Love of God
to heal thee.

*

Beloved, my angel speaks unto thy angel.
May the healing power of God
and His mighty mercy-anointing
come unto thy need.
And may the responding grace in your soul
hear and receive healing.
And may the perfect body
of your true self
sustain you,
renew you—
revitalizing,
harmonizing,
building.
And may joy return.
If there be any fear in your mind and heart,
may the blessed angels of mediation
give unto you the balm of perfect peace.

*And may the resurrection power
of the Lord Jesus
heal you.*

*

*Beloved, my angel speaks unto thy angel.
Thy faults hang loosely upon thee.
Let them go free.
And let the true Light
enter into thy heart and mind.
And be thou healed of thy fears.*

*

*Beloved, my angel speaks unto thy angel.
Love more.
Love the tender and the weak.
And call on thy angel
to heal the tender and the weak.
And thou shalt be made strong
in the Might and Power of God.*

*

*Beloved, my angel speaks unto thy angel.
I see the faith in thy heart
as a starry light—
a light which goeth not out.
And I pray
that the Will of the Father be done
in the name of His Son,
and that healing come unto thee.
Peace.*

*

Beloved, my angel speaks unto thy angel.
May the softened light of peace
ease the fevers of discontent
and still the passions of restlessness.
May your soul
center itself in the works of light fulfilled.
Beloved, I look deep into your heart
and behold its healing love.

*

Beloved, my angel speaks to thy Guardian
     Angel.
The perfect timing and the right placement
are at hand.
Be thou courageous.
And let thy heart be filled with love;
for where love is,
God verily is.

*

Beloved, my angel speaks unto thy angel.
Each man is given a very special hour
in which he learns more of God.
Therefore, I ask, if it is the Will of the Father,
may your angel come nigh unto you
and place about you an armor of light.

*

Beloved, my angel speaks unto thy angel.
Pity those who know not.
Come thou forth from thy prison house.
The door is open.

Look to peace and to freedom.
Go thou not back into thy prison place.

*

Beloved, my angel speaks unto thy angel.
If it is the Will of the Father,
may you see the world
through the eyes of perfect love;
for you are loved.

*

Beloved, my angel speaks unto thy angel.
May the little child in thee
surrender thy problems
unto Him who knoweth thy need.
And may the scars and the wounds
be healed in the name of the Christ.

*

Beloved, my angel speaks unto thy angel.
May the veil of the night
be lifted into light.
May the word spoken
become the sacred word,
healing the little self and the little will.
The true self is deathless.
Believe thou in the immortal life,
and receive thy healing quickly.
Peace.

*

Beloved, my angel speaks unto thy angel.
Look deep within,

and search thy true desiring.
Become thou not a victim
to thy weakness or the weakness of other men.
But become thou strong
in the knowing that thy soul is of God.

*

Beloved, my angel speaks unto thy angel.
All souls are ensouled in God.
And thou, beloved one,
be not bitter,
for a bitter nature
becomes a crippled spirit.
Come thou into the walk and the way,
and listen to what thy soul would say
in Christ.

*

Beloved, my angel speaks unto thy angel.
Thy soul knows only victory,
and thy soul knows the eternal patience.
Look to thy soul,
that thy mind may be illumined
and that thy unbelief
may be healed.

*

Beloved, my angel speaks unto thy angel.
Our love is as a cable
strong and true.
Many small devotions move between us,

building a love beyond the terrestrial—
a love celestial.
This is a deathless love;
this is the everlasting love—
the divine love speaking between my soul and
*   thy soul.*

*

AFTER-MEDITATION MANTRAMS

I shall cleanse away the fevers of nonsense.
And I shall cool my emotions
with pure, lucid images in thought.
I shall look for the graciousness in living,
blending with the Will of God.
I shall love more,
and therefore become more.

*

If there be any barrier
to the light in my mind,
may my thoughts come to rest
in the light of the Christ.
And may the peace of my soul
become as a healing balm.

*

May all manners of healing in the world
receive of the Great Healer.
And may I begin my devotion with love.

*May my heart be opened,
and may my eyes behold the light of truth.
May healing go unto the earth.
And may all men be blessed.*

*

*May the mighty light of my soul
blend with the light of my higher mind,
so that my True Self
may pour forth
the golden elixir.
And the renewal of Life Eternal
shall become a living verity.*

*

*My love is as a rivulet,
a small body of water,
moving towards the greater waters
of purification
and love in God.
I stand in the sun's light
blessed by the light of the day.
I look on the night and the day
and know them to be
of God.*

*

*I thank Thee, Father,
for the moments of happiness and love.
I have written them into my heart;
they shall never die.
In the days ahead,*

this memory will teach me to endure,
and to love.

＊

May I stand under grace
and look to tomorrow
with joy,
and know that each moment of the day
will reward me
in my serving in the light.

＊

Life Is.
Light Is.
Love Is.
May these three become as one in my heart
    and mind.
May I become a perfected
and worthy instrument for God.
And may I enter the door of higher instruction.

＊

I am a tryst-keeper.
I have written my name in the golden book.
The record of my works shall not die.
I shall go forth with immortal belief;
and I shall see the works of God made
    manifest.

＊

Let me learn the silent logos,
that I may speak in right timing,
and reap the fruits
of holy conversation.

*

Wherever I am sent,
may I consent.
Wherever I am placed,
may I be given the light
to erase and to dissolve my discontent.
May I fulfill my walk
with dignity, honor, truth.

*

My soul is as a stylus
writing a song—
a song of love.
My heart is a chalice,
warming in its ruby light,
healing, comforting.
My mind is a crucible
of golden, luminous light,
imaging, envisioning.
I look to the Lord of Light.
I look to the Lord of Life.
The restoring grace of my soul
giveth peace.

HEALING MANTRAMS FOR THE FAMILY

May the Guardian Angel of our home
protect us and guide us.
May we fulfill the Will of the Father,
and become more thoughtful of one another.

*

If it is the Will of the Father,
may the blessed Guardian Angel
come unto this family
so that each member
may fulfill his life purpose
as of the Will in God.
May there be healing peace and love
in this household.

HEALING MANTRAMS FOR NATIONS

O Lord, Healer and Mediator of the world,
we pray that Thou wilt heal
the men of the world.
Let men love.
And let all men come to honor, to peace.

*

In the name of the Christ,
may stalwart and true men come forth.
And may the Ambassadors of God
speak for Him in word and action.
Let men of peace in nations
receive their anointing
and uplifting
toward the light.
May the mighty Angels
and Presences of Heaven
shower upon men
ideas,
truths,
and peaceful, inspiring works.

*

When nations are sick,
men are fearful.
I pray for a new courage for men—
another vitality of courage—
that men may come to know the Ethic
of the Lord Jesus
and begin a healing work.
I pray for peace in the world.
I pray that the clamors
and the fears in the world
will come under the governings of justice,
and that men in high places
shall live within the ethic
of "Love thy neighbor as thyself."

*

Let the nations of the earth be at peace.
Let the dove take its golden talisman.
Let the hymn of praise bring freedom unto
  the earth.
And let all men join hands unto one another.
Let men know they stand in God,
and remember their works as of God.
Let the Word of the Christ speak,
and become the one tongue unto all men.

PROSPERITY OF OUR NATION

May the Angels watching over this nation
inspire each one
to fulfill the pure intent
within this national community of peoples.
May all men of this nation
be blessed of God
and sacredly prosper.

CONSECRATION OF A FLAG

May this flag be a constant reminder
of our national grace.
We dedicate our human hearts and our ethic
to the ideals as established
by the founding fathers of this nation.
May the souls of all men born in this nation
observe the ethic overdwelling this nation.

*May the Archetypal Angels who guard our
      nation
call forth great and strong men
to serve in positions of authority..
May just and merciful men
govern our nation.
May the Father preserve this nation
from weak and vacillating men.
May all men of this nation
remain close to our Father which art in
      Heaven—
the Supreme Ruler over all men.
We thank our Father in Heaven
for a right and perfect justice.
Amen.*

HEALING MANTRAMS FOR SELF

*The Divine Spirit
in His Mighty Power
is healing me.*

*

*My body is as a strong tree,
firm with good health,
harmonious with vitality.
I shall reach my roots inward
into the processes of pure living.*

And I shall send forth the branches of my
    actions
with vitality,
with peace.

*

The sifting has made me lean.
Let me value the small,
and prove to be worthy
within a new borning and beginning.

*

May my members, my organs,
become my servers.
May my love and thoughts
become mighty, illuminative
chalices for God.

*

May my standards of the past
unite with the Greater Ethic
of my spirit.

*

May the crafts of my hands
become equal to the versatility
of my spirit.

*

May the past know forgiveness.
And may the wounds that cannot be forgotten
be healed in the perfect anointing.
And may my words often say, "forgive."

And may I remember,
and walk lightly with joy.

*

I shall research my frailties.
I shall not be confused.
I shall not permit my angers
to decide my destiny.

*

I know that to endure and to forbear
is part of the way;
yet I also know
there is something beyond endurance,
beyond forbearance.
The perfect gift of grace from God
is perfect love.

*

Father, let me be not an awkward disciple.
May my rhythm and my grace become as one.

*

I will remember that courage
is a gift earned
through valiant works.

*

When I lose a physical thing,
I have offended timing.
When I fail to meet my soul's command,
I have offended God.

*

May the obstacles
which restrain me from serving God
be removed,
and the cause within these obstacles
be revealed,
so that I may know them
and face them
with truth and courage.

*

The Eternal Life and Fire within Spirit
knoweth no sickness or weakness,
destruction or fear,
lack or want,
pain or loneliness,
sorrow or departure,
going or coming—
but knoweth only the Love of Peace and Good.

SPECIAL PURPOSE MANTRAMS

FOR STRENGTH

Place unto men thy love and fear not.
Place unto men thy labors and fear not.
Place unto thy labors thy strength
and know that more strength will come unto
*   thee,*
for thou canst not famish thy strength
when thou art in the Will of God.

*

FOR WORKS

May my conscience and memory
keep chaste
my emotions,
and watch over my deeds
of this day.

*

TO OVERCOME LETHARGY

The light of God within me
is a diamond
wearing away the corrosions
of inertia.

*

FOR GUIDANCE

I believe in Divine Guidance.
I believe in spiritual healing.
I believe in the power of the Holy Ghost
    within the Word.
I believe in the Eternal One.
Now let me look into the light,
And walk in the light,
As He is in the light.

*

TO BE A GOOD STEWARD

I pity those who are penurious.
I cherish those who are reverent stewards.

The treasury of my grace
responds
to the law of reverent stewardship.

*

TO OVERCOME REGRET

The Will of God
is mighty, quick.
In the stillness
of my innermost self
the Will of God moves—
and quickens
my light,
my love.
My wounds are healed,
and order comes.

*

TO RECEIVE AN ANOINTING

May the living waters of life
heal, anoint, and bless me.
And may the dove of the Holy Ghost
descend upon me.
And may I learn of the descending and the
    ascending of the angels,
who remind me of the mighty Love of God.

*

FOR PEACE IN EMPLOYMENT

If it is the Will of the Father,
may the Guardians of Industry
bring perfect order and peace
to this environment.

＊

TO OVERCOME CONFLICT IN ORGANIZATIONS

If it is the Will of the Father,
may the Guardian Angel sustain the inherent
    expression
of this .... (group, fraternal
    organization or institution).
And may all engaged in the labors herein
become benefactors to the world.

＊

TO SET ARIGHT ESTRANGEMENT

My sympathies seek
to be more compassionate each day.
Today I shall fill my heart
with tenderness
and understanding,
for I would heal
the wounds of separateness.

＊

DEDICATION TO HEAL

May my healing ministry begin.
And may I blend with the Mending Angels.
May my body become a worthy vessel,
a holy temple of pure peace.

●

TO CHANNEL THE REAL

In light I reveal the real.
In love I stand.
In sending forth I heal.
In healing I blend.
Unto those who seem not to know or to blend,
    I give;
And in giving, I forgive.
In love I stand.
I stand within the eternal plan of love in God.

✱

TO STAND IN LIGHT

I stand as a blessed one;
and the events of my life bless each one.
I stand as a lighted one;
and my lighted actions light the way.
I stand as a golden one;
and my golden ways of love and expectations
    give the golden enlightenment onto men.

✱

TO SPEAK TRUE

Every word I speak
is a creation.
Let my words be high,
pure,
loving.
If I cannot speak pure words,
let me await my time for speaking.

*

TO SEE IN RIGHT PROPORTION

Today I make a covenant
to observe the ethic of proportion;
to see the beautiful beyond the sordid;
to hear only the harmony
and not the raucous;
to speak truth,
knowing it to be deathless;
to feel with reverence;
to avoid the vulgar;
to trust and trust again and again
beyond doubt.

*

TO HEAL CHILDREN

O children,
whose feet stumble in the world,
my half-said prayers
pray for thee.

*Come unto the homeplace
of the Father.
Let Him take thee as sons
and direct thee.
I pray for weak children,
for sick children,
for confined children.
I pray for hungry children and illiterate
    children.
I praise God Who healeth all.*

*

TO ERASE THE PAST

*Let the memory of the old
become the power of the now.
And let the power of the now
absolve the sorrows of the past.
Let the scattering winds of passion,
and the soiled waters of sorrow,
be collected into rivers of undisturbed going
    and becoming.
Let passion's plan have its perfect coverlet
    in peace.
Let the old spendings become the new in
    sendings.
Let the two in very part of me
become the one in every part of God.*

Consecrating myself to the last mile
and to the last hour of activity,
I slough off the darkened actions of the
    decaying past.
Freely standing in Light, I stand forth in
    Christ.

*

TO DEDICATE A NEW HOME

May the Guardian Angel of this home
overdwell and protect our coming and going.
And may this home be lighted
with true hospitality.
May each meal be a holy agape.
May those who enter here honor this home,
and be honored.
We dedicate our home to the Presence of God.

*

TO UNITE WITH THE LOVE OF JESUS

O Master, O Lord,
let men seek Thee.
O Lord of Love,
let men who know Thee
return to Thee.
Thy Love, O Lord,
doth encompass and heal me.
O Lord Jesus, let Thy Love
heal this eternity.

FASTING MANTRAMS

May the Lord of Love anoint me.

*May I become a healing instrument for the
world.*

*I give thanks unto Thee; I give thanks unto
Thee, O Eternal.*

*May this fast prepare me for a continuing holy
ministry.*

*May my hands be anointed, and may my body
be healed, so that I may become a holy
channel for the healing of men in the
world.*

*

*I anoint my head with the desire for humility,
humbleness, sincerity, simplicity.*

May I be a truth-sayer and a good-doer.

*May this fast bring peace to the fiery tensions
within my will.*

*May my struggles give me the power of
endurance.*

*And may my soul give me the power to
overcome.*

*And may endurance and overcoming enable
me to hear clearly what the inner ear would
hear.*

*I pray unto the Father that the fast of this day
shall be a sacred and spiritual fast.*

*

*God has inspired my heart as to the meaning
of prayer, devotion, fasting.*

*May I serve Him with devotion. And may this
day's fasting and the hopes lying close to
my heart become audible in good works.*

*May this fast anoint me and still the confused
fragments of my thinking.*

May my senses be cleansed and purged.

*May I fulfill, in every manner, the pattern and
the plan of God.*

*If it is the Will of the Father, may my sacred
key, my sacred word, and my sacred tone
become as one; for I would speak of God.*

*May this fast purify my speaking; and may my
words become a part of the greater Word
or Creation of God.*

*

*May I be surrounded by the Ministering
Angels on this day.*

May my serving blend with the world-need.

*And may my presumptuous sins be revealed
unto my mind, that I may better serve and
better work in the world.*

*May my hopes be set upon a true destiny
whereby mankind will be bettered.*

*May my small and large works be
accomplished.*

*May my good intent and my efforts become as
one for Christ.*

I receive this anointing with humility.
May my restless will come to rest in the Will
of God.

*

Father, I pray to do Thy Will.
I pray to think not of myself as burdened.
I pray to think of myself in a state of
bountifulness—protected and blessed.
May this fast help me to understand the true
surrender unto Thy Will.

*

May the Eternal Spirit, the Divine Spirit, and
the Holy Spirit shower their blessings
upon me.
May this sacred fast still my fears.
And may my thoughts and love combine as
holy emotions for God.
May the book of my soul's record be read
fearlessly, lovingly.
And may my works imprinted thereon be sty-
lused in golden light; for I would that my
word and works become at one with the
Word of God.
May the creative word be spoken in my
thoughts and emotions.
And may all fears be removed, that I may be
healed of my fears and partake of the
Holy Spirit.

*

*On this day of fasting I pray that men may
recover the dignity of craftsmanship, of
serving, of inspiration and creation.*

*I dedicate this fast to creation, to inspiration,
and to all things created out of the souls
of men.*

*May I use the wisdom within each lesson and
each event, and create with joy.*

*If I have failed to create with joy, I have left
a dark mark upon existence. If I have
created with wisdom, I have left a golden
mark upon life—and my soul shall sing.*

*Blessed are those who create for God. May I
commune with them through my soul's
knowing.*

*And may I be ever in an holy company of
persons seeking to be creatively perfected,
and to work as creators with God.*

*

*May my lips be unbound, and may my words
become free with praise-giving for God.*

*May I take up my yoke with willingness—the
yoke of discipline.*

*May my eyes be opened, and may I overcome
the darkened vision.*

*I shall think only on praises to God on this
day of fasting.*

*My praises shall overflow; and my garment of
  love shall be free to love, to give.*
And my thoughts shall become holy, inspired.

*

*May this fast be a fast of peace, a fast of
  anointing, loving, giving.*
May the inner harmony quieten my fears.
*And may my courage, stamina, and sustaining
  remove the veil of doubt and tension.*
*May each moment of this anointed day be a
  holy moment of inner illumination, understanding, and grace.*
*And may the words of my lips, the love in my
  heart, and the serving of my hands become
  as one for the grace of God.*
*Whatever the hours of this day may bring,
  may I meet it with courage and joy.*

*

*May this fast be a fast of purification and
  restoring.*
*May the mighty power of God resolve and
  dissolve all things which stand between
  me and the Will of God.*
*May my own perfect body, my perfect mind,
  and my perfect heart be at one on this day.*
*And may I learn of my perfect mind, my
  perfect heart.*
*May the veil between me and the real be
  opened.*

*May I see each small thing and each greater
    thing as part of the Plan and the Will.
And may I also consecrate myself to mighty
    prayers on this day.
I thank Thee, Father.*

PRE-SLEEP MANTRAMS

*My happiness is dependent upon the freedom
of my soul. Each night I pray that my serving
shall provide a greater range for my soul's
work in both night and day.*

*

*The clouds of the day are stilled in the mid-
night of sleep. Peace, O my soul; tomorrow is
another perfect, bright day for the works of God.*

*

*Let my judging thoughts come to rest on this
night. May I learn the joy of Holy Comparison
and see all things in perfect rightness.*

*

*There is a threshold, a place, a tryst for this
night. I shall arise to the tryst designated by
my soul.*

*

*I pray to find a quiet solace, a rest beyond sleep;
for I would awaken ready to meet tomorrow's
challenge.*

*

I shall count my responsibles as joy; I shall not take my burdens into sleep.

*

I can do mighty works with the Father. Let me think on the unceasing adjustment, balance, and equanimity to be gained through mediation.

*

My freeing grace giveth to me a way. My anointing grace drieth my tears. My valor grace giveth armor for my trials. My freeing grace cometh from my release of those I love. My anointing grace cometh from my merciful deeds. My valor grace cometh from enduring and overcoming.

*

Tonight before sleeping I shall contemplate the pearls of my day. My grateful heart shall lift me beyond the gravity portals of sleep.

*

The Light of the night is a healing Light. The Light of the night is a holy Light. My prayers go up and up into the Light of the night.

*

The smallest seed contains a tone of creation. The mightiest star resounds the harmony of God. I shall sleep again with joy.

*

I am convinced that my angels do watch over me—sustain me in the night, in the day, and in all manners. I know the angels are never far from me.

*

The season of the years, months, days, the hours and moments of my inner world—all speak to me of expanding, of becoming. Let me move with the tide and become a true swimmer in the river of life.

*

May the sleeping many find repose in healing dreams. May the servers of this night be heavenly routed upward by their angels of the night.

*

Timing is of the music in Heaven; let me keep step with the march of the valiant ones who have heard the angels and know their musics.

*

Many who see in part have said that sleep is but a little death, knowing not the deathless and timeless way; for the soul sleepeth not, in sleep or in death. I am of the soul, eternally awake to God.

*

Only I can chastise my will. God punisheth not, neither doth His Law accuse. The Love of God is Perfect. The Will of God is Mighty. God has given me a will to correct my straying senses. He has given me a way and a heart to receive His Love.

*

Kings and clods and beggars—these all rest in sleep. And their angels nigh, speak of oneness.

*

If I have only one ministry and it is of hope, the angels shall guide my way toward confirming verities; and healing truths shall manifest for God.

*

I am a receiver of blessings beyond lip telling. I am a blessed one; for God has given unto me a lamp to keep, and a Light to behold.

*

My happiness comes from acceptance, application, and effort. My sleep tonight is a pause for instruction. May I better learn the little rules, and thus come to receive both the smaller and the greater blessings of Heaven.

*

My soul-cry is heard in Heavenly corridors, where resideth the Recording Angels. My Guardian Angel shall send the answer to my cry, and I shall recover the splendor of true ways and right works.

*

All of my urges are tendrils reaching for light. All of my struggles are compass needles pointing the way to creation.

*

Heaven is reached through selfless acceptance. Heaven is observed through pure eyes. Heaven

is experienced when angels come nigh unto the
soul's need.

*

May my sleeping body receive the balm of
Gilead sent forth from the Healers of the night.

*

If I be reckless with my days, I shall become
my own adversary. My soul has revealed that
a wanton way is an accumulative circle ever
repeating and adding to. May I come forth into
the upward spiral of perfect hopes and healing
helps; for time waits not for one who respects
not time.

*

The Saints of Heaven—so nigh to the rainbow
splendors of good men—each night send their
love, their helps to those who believe, who pray.

*

May I resolve my opinions hampering the rise
of the angelic pinions near by; for "I can of
mine own self do nothing . . . the Father that
dwelleth in me, He doeth the works."

*

How may I define God, save I look unto His
canopy of worlds, universes, stars, galaxies.
How may I define my world, save I know God
is centered in my own expanding way.

THE END

INDEX

A

Aaron's rod 215
Abraham 68,82,115
adultery 147,153
agnostic 3,160,161,219
all-genesis 73,176
Alpha-tones 22,27,32,34,35,39,56,57,60-62,66,69,176,181
alternates 18,40,45,46,52,55,179-181,210,211
Ancient of Days 100
androgynous 66,69
Angel(s) 7-9,16,17,23,26,28,36,39,41,46,47,51,55,60,61,
    63,64,85,86,89,94,97,105,120-122,124,128,129,132,137,
    142-144,159,167,172,176,180,198,204,205,213,235,241,
    245,255,256,262,274-277
        Agrarian 142
        Archetypal 256
        Celestial 46
        Cherubim 46,230
        Death 208
        Fertility 63
        Flora 63
        Great Deva 63
        Guardian (see Guardian Angel)
        Judgment 8,69,71,72,80,83,86,89
        Luciferic 41,162
        Luminosity 46,133
        Mending 264
        Ministering 204,269
        Niscience 46,133
        of Chastity 184
        of Hope 201
        of Pure Desiring 46,133
        Pollinating 63
        Procreation 46,68,80,88
        Propagation 76,88,89,127,142,184
        Recording (see Recording Angel)
        Species 36,65
        Succoring 204
        Terrestrial 36,46
Angel to Angel Mantrams 239,243-250
animals 16,36,47,54,59,61-65,70,71,75,84,164,165
antichrist 202
apostle 106,177
Archangels 39,40,45,46,52,53,63,101,105

archetype(s) 13,30,36,39,42,46,53,72,84,86,173,175,200,229
art 231
astral regions 219
atheism 161
atom(s) 31,33,34,38,42,45,50,51,53,56,57,60,68,69,109-111,
    114,210
        axis 35,58,71
        cosmos 31-36,40,45,58-62,66,69,71,100
        emotional 109,110
        eternal 39,56
        eternal sustaining 38-42,45,57
        family (see family-atom)
        mental 49,50,133,219
        sacred 63,67,75,102,106,133,181,193,195
        sentient 49,109,228
        tribal (see tribal-atom)

B

bacteria 33,56,190,192,210
baptism 180
beauty 134,243
Being(s) 21,23,29,53,101,114,196
beliefs 194
Benjamin 117
Bible 26,67,68,79,100,105,187
birth 14,15,18,19,22,42,45,52,56,59
blood 27,37,46,47,50,51,56,66,108,122,124,130,167,180,184,
    187,190,197,210,211,218
bones 182,218
brain 51
brother 126,132,147,148,184,187,193
builder(s) 10,12,13,27

C

cannibalism 72,78,160
celibacy 150,153,155
cell(s) 6,27,37,56,66,196,210,211,216,218,226
charitableness 11,167
chemicals 15,16,47
Cherubim Angels 46,230
Christ 1,3,4,9,10,15,25,40,45,62,74,101-106,133,174,201,
    236,243,245,248-250,257
        Light 1,15,173,200,240
        Mind 133,170,173,187,217

Christ Spirit 24,29,30,46,52,73,102,103,106,157,174,178,
       200,201
children 28,31,50,68,70,72,73,76,83,90,95,117,118,122,125,
       127-129,132,137,140-151,164,165,184,187,188,213,
       265,266
co-atom 29,57,133,237
conscience 7-9,41,75,76,81,88,97-99,133,158-167,171,201,
       202,230,261
       family 8,121,123-126,158,160,162-165,171,214
       national 160
       racial 8,158,160
       religious 158,160
       tribal 76,114,158,160,161,163,164
       world 5,9,13,157,158,160,171,214
consciousness 17,20,21,23,35,53-61,65,73-75,102,109,111,
       161,168,181,187,209
constellation(s) 99,101,102
contemplation 235
continent(s) 3,5,13,14,71,94,138
cosmic birth 18,19,21,23,33,53-55,66,77,82,87,118,133,141,
       173,183,184,200,201,205
       death 23
       energy 25
       sleep 23
cosmos 18,19,22,23,31,40,61
       atom(s) 31-36,40,45,58-62,66,69,71,100
       genesis 57,73,104,137,170,172,174,175
craftsman 10,13,14,17,94,190
craftsmanship 9,271
creation 9-11,17,20,21,25-27,31,33,39,68,69,78,101,104,137,
       150,180,210,218,231,234,243,269,271
culture 27,114,231
cursing 80

                      D

David 83
death 18,22,46,48,55,57,58,83,126,133,183,188,203,275
       angel of 208
de-manifestation 20,23,32,51,86,216
destiny 2
destroying principle 46,86
disciples 105,174,213,259
disease 203,206
Divine Spirit 4,29,174,175,225,257,270
divorce 151-154

dreams 97,98,124-126,132,161,202,203
dweller 86,122,123,126,128,172

E

Eden 67
    semi- 70,71
Edenic 39,49,75,157,210
education 107,130
egotistical shell 163,164,169,172,207,219
Elect 6,17,68
electrical 26,41,49,223
electricity 58
elementals 76
emotion(s) 6,26,27,37,41,46,49,51,55,57
emotional body 44,46-50,55,57,108-112,121,158,208,220,221
    atom(s) 110
encasement, etheric 32,33,57,59-62,66,69,77,78,86,87,89,
    104,126,127,154,192
energy 31,35,39,46-49,51,59,60,67,98,192,223
enlightenment 2
Enoch 68
entities 219
Equation, God's 17,18,22,60,61,89,201,203-206,218,229
Esau 82
Essenes 118
Eternal life 38,42,251,260
    One 4,6,12,14,43,94,261
    Spirit 16,18,29,65,66,189,200,206,227,229,270
    sustaining atom 38-42,45,57
ether 31,67,69,183
etheric 37,44,70,157
    body 29,44,46-50,55,57,133,208-211,222-224
ethic(s) 6,9,10,13,57,113,122,131,132,158,160,162,166,169,
    173,174,180,187,189,192,197,201-203,205-207,212,217,
    224,227,238,255,256,258,265
    Jesus 26,29,158,177,179,182,191,215
everlasting body 46,48,49
evil 7,8,17,28,52,86,160,201
exercise 197

F

faith 26,28,128,184-186,188,193-196,204,229,230,238,239
family-atom 73,86,87,115,117,118,120,122,124-135,139,140,
    142,144,148,150,152,153,155,162,172,174,184,185,187
    fixed 119

grace 119,121
family-genesis 73,81,84,87,96-100,104-108,110,111,115,
    117-120,124,125,127,132,138,144,145,152,154,157,162,
    166,167,172,174,184,236
Fasting Mantrams 268-273
flag 256
foods 142-144,183,192,197,198,208,227
friend 151,181
friendship 165,166

G

generation 36,37,47,67,68,72,81,83,96,104,121
genius 142,168
glands 36,53,66,143,157,210,216
God, Equation of 17,18,22,60,61,89,201,203-206,218,229
    grace of 225,272
    Kingdom of 42,230
    Law of 8,17,25,113,146,155,159,162,164,201-203,216,
        224,225
    Love of 1,8,17,113,201,203,217,220,221,245,262
    Plan of 19,20,28,94,95,139,169
    Presence of 267
    Son of 15,27,29,178,200
    Spirit of 4,6,17,18,31,44,102,181,218
    Word of 14,17,178,202,241
good 7-9,52,121,130,159,160,184,200,205,212,230,244,260
grace 11,12,51,64,79,119,121,124-129,132,138,141,142,147,
    154,172,188,198,205,212,223,226,227,235-237,252,
    259,262,272,274
    anastasis 209
    family-atom 119
    healing 195,238
    national 256
    restoring 206
gravity 30,36,37,40,41,44,47,53,56-58,65,66,75,157,181
Great Beings 53
    Immortals 230
Guardian Angel(s) 9,46,72,82,120-122,132,159,161,198,
    199,236,247,263,276
        family 9,120-128,132,172
        home 254,267
        nation 236
        race 69,76,77,86
        tribal 9,75,76,82,95
Guardians of Industry 263

guidance 77,121,125,126,132,167,197,254,261
guilt 122,159,168,202,213,214,221

H

hands, laying on of 222-224
healers 11,13,29,177,179,180,197,199,202,204,206,220,228,
    229,235-237
    Mediative (see Mediative Healers)
healing 28,79,130,141,173,177,182,190-196,198,199,201,
    203,205,207,211-224,226,229,233-238,250,261,264,277
    Cloisters of Heaven 232,233
    grace 238
    mantrams for family 254
            for nations 254-257
            for self 257-260
    mediative (see mediative healing)
Heaven 5,13,24,28,30,41,44-46,73,94,99,110,120,138,198,
    203,205,213,218,219,230,231,236,275-277
    Kingdom of 16
    music of 240,242
    Presences of 255
herbs 197,198
Hierarch(s) 13,22,24,25,29,36,39,40,45,49,50,52,55-57,
    65-69,72,73,99-103,105,111,133,175,176
higher etheric body 46,48-50,55,57,208-210,222,223
    self 111,209
    worlds 117
Holy Ghost 160,261,262
    of Holies 157
    Presences 16,39,45,48,50,51,73,164,205,235,255
    Spirit 270
homes 140-146,150,155,267
homosexuality 161
hospitality 155,162
Host 101,209
human-genesis (see family-genesis)
human spirit 1-15,24,30,43,64,69,70,72,73,84,85,88,94,99,
    136,137,157,180,182,187,190,193,200,201,210
humility 166,171
husband 127,128,141,145-147,150,152

I

ideas 13,47,52,53,55,74,105,137,255
illumination 272
imaging 2,13,20,21,45,47,50,52,66,158,176

indestructible atom 106
individualistic atom 75,107,108-112,114,121,167,168
individuality 73,74,79,110,111,119,131,167,168,171,174,185
initiation(s) 27,28,48.55,60,82,96,106,110,115,131,133,137,
    138,158,167,179-191,193,205,207,211,218,237
inspiration 11,271
interior worlds 72
interracial marriage 88,89
intuition 11,14,185,222
invisible sun 103
invisible worlds 237
inward self 224,227,232
Isaac 115

J

Jacob 81-83,105,115,116,174
Jehovah 5,67-71,86,100
        Race-Guardian Angels 75
        Recording Angels 76
Jesus Ethic 26,29,158,177,179,182,191,215
Job 176,187-190
Joseph (father of Jesus) 118,119
        (son of Jacob) 116,117
joy 2,20,113,117,140,142,175,176,178,179,271
Judgment Angels 8,69,71,72,80,83,86,89
Jupiter 134

K

karma 88-90,103,119,120,123,126,128,130,140,172,173
Kingdom of God 42,230
        of Heaven 16
knowledge 12,21,54,83

L

language 94,95,141
Law(s) of God 8,17,25,113,146,155,159,162,164,201-203,
    216,224,225
Life-tone(s) 24,25,39,52
Light of Christ 1,15,173,200,240
Light-tone(s) 24,25,52
lives, previous 123,125,148,150,152,154,155,168,211,213,
    214,219,222,228,235
logic 169
logos 13,94,157,217,235,253
Lord of Love 47,56,150,268

Lucifer 41,175
    Angels 41,162
lungs 37,41,182

M

magnetism 26,41,49,58,197,207,223
manifestation 20,83,150,216,224,226,229
mantramic speaking 208,235
Mantrams
    After-meditation 250-253
    Angel to Angel 239,243-250
    Before-meditation 239-243
    Fasting 268-273
    Healing, family 254
             nations 254-257
             self 257-260
    Pre-sleep 273-277
    Special purpose 260-267
marriage 88-90,115,116,118,123,126-128,130,136-138,
         145-147,150-155,187
    interracial 88,89
Mars 133,134
Mary 118,119
medallion of the soul 153,215
mediation 5,16,20-22,28,36,45,51,55,98,100-102,113,123,
         132,164,170,174,176,180,191,195,208,235,241,245
Mediative Healer(s) 191,196-199,218-220,223-226,228,
                     235-238
             healing 191,193,196-199,202,205,211,213,
                     218-228,235-239
medical science 191,192
medicine 192,197,229,236
meek 56,57,60,61,176
Melchizedek 175
memory(ies) 20,21,23,24,37,44,50,52,56,71,88,96,97,101,
         108,122,124,125,182,261,266
mental atoms 49,50,133,219
         body 44,46-50,55,56,109,112,167,168,208
Mercury 135
mercy 11,26,54,78,114,120,159,179,182,190-193,195,199,
         201,204,206,220,229,245,274
Messiah 118
metaphysicians 229,236
minerals 16,36,47,59,192
miracles 17,94,147,177,191,201,207,229,242

285

moon 23,35,36,58,67,100
moral(s) 86,122,125,130,131,152,159,182,201,203,238
Moses 37,86,151
mother 123,125-127,129,132,142-145,148,151,184
mountains 71,183
music 18,31,231,232,275
     of Heaven 240,242

N

nation(s) 5,13,15,85-87,95,100,107,108,138,158,159,172,
    191,192,236,254-257
Nature 46,54,58,76,84,114,197,208
    Spirits 76,216
Neptune 135
New Testament 105,171
Night Ministry 223
Niscience Angel 46,133
Noah 68
nomadic-genesis (see tribal-genesis)
nutrition 197,231

O

Old Testament 68,88,105,171
Omega-tones 27,28,32,57,58,61,63,176
omniscient cell 133
one-genesis 73,176

P

pain 8,10,14,15,46,81,163,175,178,180,182,183,195,209,211,
    215,216,224,225,236,260
    octave of 79,174,175,177-182
patience 114,128,152,249
Paul 82
peace 4,52,160,178,179,190,204,230-233,236,260
personality 74,79,80,104,108-112,135,167,170,173
Peter 82
philosopher(s) 11,18
physician 192,197,198,229
planet(s) 3,23,26,34-36,38,49,53,58-60,71,99,101,133,134
plants 16,29,36,38,47,59,62,63,65,70,183,192,198
Pluto 135
polarity(ies) 13,41,42,53,66,67,136,138
polygamy 83,88
prayer(s) 29,118,123,128-130,147,193-196,207,208,212,219,
    221,222,225,226,231,235,239,277

Presences, Holy 16,39,45,48,50,51,73,164,205,235,255
Pre-sleep Mantrams 273-277
procreation 68,81,117,118,121,172
pro-genesis 43,73,74,172,175,176
propagation 68,69,116,157
prophets 26,96,105
psychiatry 98,236
purgatory 230
purity 205,216

R

race(s) 5,15,67-70,76,77,80,85-87,89,90,99,100,103,107,138,
        158,170,172,191,192,236
rebirth 18,54,60
Recording Angel(s) 8,26,46,69,75,86,122,126,127,132,159,
                    172,186,194,198,199,202,229,276
    family 120-123,126-128,132,172
re-embodiment 84,87,89,110,118
reincarnation 76,84,87-89,100,102-105,107,173
religion(s) 95,96,107,114,122,130,131,149,158,159,162,169,
        170,172
repentance 202,212,221
resurrection 55,179,240,246
retribution 71,83,95,107
reverence 50,79,108,109,113,123,127,128,134,135,142,147,
        169,170,179,184-186,189,195,205,212,222
ritual(s) 122,127,183

S

sacrament 13
Saints 205,230,277
Satan 41,150,188,202
Saturn 134,178
Saviour 118
science 4,21,22,26,34,138,139,144,169,191,192,201,206,
        229,236
scientist(s) 10-13
seer 26
self-genesis 73,74,85,89,96-99,103,105,106,110,112,132,135,
        136,139,144-147,152-154,159,161,163-174,185,186,207,
        219,228
selflessness 167,171
semi-Eden 70,71
Seraphim 46,230
sex 78,80,107,123,146,150,153,155,173,183-186,216

shepherd(s) 10-13
sickness 51,81,99,124,129,162,187,188,192-194,196,203-205,
    207-210,213-215,219,224,255,260
Simon the magician 207
sin(s) 14,25,122,214,220-222
sister 126,132,147,148,184,187
skin 37,38,67
skull 98
sleep 48,72,133,159,175,209,274,275,277
society 6,27,114,140,149,158,159,168,172,181,184,228
Solomon 83,84
Son of God 27,29,52,178,200
Son of Man 55,207
speech 21,95
spine 215
Spirit 19,72
    Divine 4,29,174,175,225,257,270
    Eternal 16,18,29,65,66,189,200,205,206,227,229,270
    Holy 270
    Life 43
    of God 4,6,17,18,31,44,102,181,218
spiritual gifts 172,173
        life 102,110,119,131,171,172,174,188
        worlds 58,68,98,110,174,238
star(s) 99,176
stewardship 120,123,141,187,189,190,205,261,262
stigmata 211,212
stomach 143
sun(s) 23,26,31,34-36,38,58-60,71,99,100,113,176,178,
        192,208
    invisible 103
surgery 197,198
symbology 94-99,125,143

                    T

talent(s) 131,134,136,168,178,189,203
teacher 11
teaching 173
telepathy 47,148
Ten Commandments 86
tenderness 11,17,206,245,263
third vitality 229
timing 5,15,19,53,62,89,107,129,132,148,204,211,212,236,
    237,243,247,253,259,275

tone(s) 31
      Alpha- 22,27,32,34,35,39,56,57,60-62,66,69,176,181
      creative 13
      Life- 24,25,39,52
      Light- 24,25,52
      Omega- 27,28,32,57,58,61,63,176
trees 182
tribal-atom(s) 77,78,86,114,120,173
tribal-genesis 73-77,80-85,88,95,98-100,104-106,108,110,111,
    114-118,126,171,172,174,236
tribe(s) 5,69,71-79,85-87,90,95,96,100,103,104,107,108,111,
    114,116,119,138,142,157,158,164,167,174,183,184,
    191,192
truth(s) 11,12,52,53

      U

Uranus 135

      V

Venus 134,135
vibratory hum 153,154
virtues 231
void 33,34,39,56,60
   living 32

      W

war(s) 3,5,8,76,107,108,180,224,226
wife 127,128,132,141,146,147,150,152
wisdom 11,12,15,17,53,79,131,195,230,237,271
Word 157,178,179,181,240,257,261,269
world conscience 5,9,13,157,158,160,171,214
worlds, higher 117
      interior 72
      invisible 237
      of God 74
      subtle 220
worship 72,77,96,114,122,160,168,170,189
world-soul atom 34-36,39,58-60,67,99-104,106,114,115,173

BOOKS AND LESSONS
by Ann Ree Colton

BOOKS

WATCH YOUR DREAMS
An invaluable and necessary book revealing the soul-codes in dreams and their symbols.

ETHICAL E S P
An important book defining the difference between lower and higher ESP

THE JESUS STORY
A miracle book in timing to the need for miracles.

THE HUMAN SPIRIT
A scientific, spiritual, and healing book on the creation, purpose and destiny of man.

PROPHET FOR THE ARCHANGELS
The life story of Ann Ree Colton.

THE SOUL AND THE ETHIC
A profound book on the soul and on the etheical use of soul power.

THE KING
From the personal, hieroglyphic journal of Ann Ree Colton.

DRAUGHTS OF REMEMBRANCE
An extraordinary book on the subject of reincarnation.

MEN IN WHITE APPAREL
A book of vital revelations about death and the life after death.

THE VENERABLE ONE
An initiatory book for those who love Nature and who would unveil Nature's secrets.

VISION FOR THE FUTURE
A prophetic book to comfort men in a perilous time.

THE LIVELY ORACLES
A prophetic book on world events.

ISLANDS OF LIGHT
A book of initiation with an underlying prophetic theme.

PRECEPTS FOR THE YOUNG
Appreciated by the adult . . . inspiring to the child . . . and beneficial to the family.

MONTHLY LESSONS
Personalized home-study lessons. Complete philosophical, practical and spiritual instruction.

BOOK *by* Jonathan Murro

GOD-REALIZATION JOURNAL
A book opening a new world of understanding related to the Presence of God.

ARC PUBLISHING CO.
P.O. Box 1138   Glendale, California 91209